The fuzzy-headed fivesome—Derek, Allan, Woody, Leslie and Eric—Britain's most sensational pop group since the coming of the Beatles, have now burst on the American music scene like comets.

Their records sell in the millions and their fan club gets a truckload of letters every day.

Quite simply, they've become a legend.

Now, for the first time, Tam Paton and the boys tell the full heartwarming story of their struggle to the top—in the only official biography of

The
Bay City
Rollers

THE BAY CITY ROLLERS

Tam Paton with Michael Wale

A BERKLEY MEDALLION BOOK
published by
BERKLEY PUBLISHING CORPORATION

THE BAY CITY WHO?

It was a face I couldn't get out of my mind. I think it was the honest cheekiness about it. It belonged to a fourteen-year-old boy and it peered up at me regularly on the stage of the Palais de Danse in Edinburgh. It belonged to Alan Longmuir, the first member of The Bay City Rollers I was to meet.

It was a funny way for such a story to start, really, because I was the leader of The Tam Paton Orchestra at the time, and we had this weekly teenage night. It was just as groups were beginning to come in, and big bands like mine beginning to go out.

Anyway, halfway through the evening there used to be this other band who'd fill in for us. The big revolve would swing round and suddenly we'd be backstage on our break. And it was during these breaks that I really began to get to know Alan and find out about his aspirations and ambitions for the future. Little was I to know then that not only would all these aspirations and ambitions come true, but that I would be involved in them as well.

I used to go up and have a coffee on the balcony overlooking the dance floor, and one night the same cheeky face I'd seen from the stage arrived at my table. Because I'd seen him so often, it was almost as if I knew him already, so it was no surprise really that we were soon chatting quite freely .

Alan said he'd got a group and that his brother was in it as well, and he asked me if I would like to hear them. Well, what do you say? In my position in those days, quite a few people used to come and ask me if I'd like to hear this or that group because I did some booking as well as running my own orchestra. Still, I did promise him that when I had a moment I would come down and see his band and meet his brother.

Oddly enough, it was after a decision that in future the Palais would no longer run its own big band that I became more interested in Alan's plans.

We realized we should get a group in instead of our own orchestra and I got the job of picking which groups would appear. They had to be young, and they had to be in the starting-out stage, because we were only paying about six pounds a time.

To be honest, I told Alan I'd be interested in coming to see his group simply to get rid of him. It had become a regular thing on a Thursday night. He'd come along with some of his mates, and sit next to me when I was having my coffee and they'd all talk about music and ask me questions and things like that. Well, I'd been in music most of my life and I was on my break and often I'd prefer to talk about something else. After all, at the time it was my job.

Anyway, as I've said, I did promise to go and see Alan and his brother and their group, and I always keep a promise. But this was one promise I almost broke through a genuine mistake. I was very friendly with Stuart Henry, the disc jockey, and I'd already promised him that I'd go to Glasgow with him on the night I'd said I would see the Longmuirs. It wasn't until we'd reached the outskirts of Edinburgh that I suddenly remembered where I should have been. I told Stuart all about the group and I blurted out: 'God what will they think of me? They'll say he's just another person who isn't really interested.' I remember thinking that missing out on seeing them would really finish it all, and I'd never hear from them again. But luckily that wasn't the case.

The following night Alan phoned me at my house. As I lived just a little way outside Edinburgh, I said I would drive into town straight away. Alan said he would rush round and get his group together.

He lived in a tenement flat on the ground floor and I was ushered in by his mother. The group were all set up ready to play in the back room. It was a very neat little back room and they looked a neat collection of young people.

So I sat there on a chair and they started to play.

Well, Beatle stuff was all the rage then, and that was what they played. The song, 'Mister Postman', especially stuck in my mind because they played it with great energy, which seemed to say a lot about the potential of the group.

As for the rest, to be quite honest, it didn't sound too good. It was their keenness, more than anything, that impressed me. It was as if they wanted to do nothing else but make it to the top. That might sound a little bit silly now when you read it in cold print, but believe me, there are plenty of people in our business who just don't have that willpower. They either crack when the strain of fighting for success gets too much or drop out when their work starts interfering with their private lives; yet here was this group of young guys who were still at school, and yet quite determined that they were going to make it.

A year or two later I was to think very often, as we went through really hard times together, that it would be this absolute will to win that would see us all through. And in the end it did. But it took a long time. They always said it took The Beatles eight years to become an overnight success. Well, it didn't take The Rollers eight years, but I think it took more than that off my life at times.

Looking back, I don't know why the boys ever picked me to guide them. After all, I was only a band leader at the local Palais. I wasn't a big, successful manager or anything like that. I think they probably thought I could get them a job at the Palais.

Sitting in that tiny room in Alan's tenement home, I remember thinking how ridiculous the whole thing was. The group had these very small amplifiers, and there were six of them in the group in those days. In fact, they told me very seriously that they'd only just changed their name to The Bay City Rollers – they had been called The Saxons before that. It sounded funny coming from the mouths of these very young boys. And like everything they did, they were very serious about it all.

When I went back to my job at the Palais I told a bloke who managed a very successful Edinburgh group called The Beachcombers that I might manage The Rollers. I asked him to listen to them and give me his opinion because, after all, he was a successful manager, and I was only a singer at the Palais.

I took him down to the tenement flat and we both sat there and listened while the boys played. And when we got back in the car the chap said: 'They've no chance. You're wasting your time. They'll never make it.'

I think it was precisely because he reacted in such a way that I was determined that they should make it. I saw the chap as a rival really. There had always been this thing between the two of us and that was that.

From that moment on I became the manager of The Bay City Rollers.

The first thing I had to do was to get them some work, because they had hardly any equipment. It was really quite sad as we trailed around all these clubs trying to get bookings and getting turned down because no one had heard of us.

Luckily, I knew quite a few managers of clubs, but you had to be a group like The Beachcombers to get into the places I wanted The Bay City Rollers to play. Still, we did at last get a slight start at a place called The Top Storey Club. It was run by two brothers, Jimmy and Russell Craig, and I asked them to book The Rollers. It was a hard job persuading them because they'd never heard of the boys in their lives; but eventually they did agree to give us a job one Sunday night – for the princely sum of five pounds. That was what the payment was for that sort of night.

That was the first gig The Rollers played under my management and it came about one week after I had taken over.

When the great day arrived, the boys were obviously very excited. I was just that bit nervous. I realized it was an important start to our relationship together. The Top Storey Club, as its name implies, was on the top floor of a tall building over Burtons down Leith Walk in Edinburgh. They've knocked it all down since, and I believe there's a hotel there now.

The deal was that The Bay City Rollers would play for about two and a half hours. And it was a night I won't forget in a hurry, because they repeated their numbers at least three times – if not more. You see, in those days they didn't know that many tunes, and as this was their first big gig they just didn't have the music to fill all the time. It was all a bit ghastly. The audience didn't sit down and listen – they just danced to the music. One or two girls stood at the front of the stage, but that was all. Definitely a night to forget as far as I was concerned.

It was after that gig that the boys officially appointed me

their manager. Which was a bit funny really. I'd taken it for granted that I was their manager!

It happened as we sat outside the club in this old van the boys had got. We talked until five in the morning. I can tell you we were getting a bit cold by then. Firstly, they all sat there and listened to what I had to say, and then we all had a good old chat. In fact it was just starting to get light when Alan suddenly asked me: 'Would you like to be manager of the group?' I said: 'Yeah. We'll see how it works out.'

So then I really became interested and started phoning all around the place trying to get the group work. But people kept saying: 'It's nice to hear your voice, Tam, but who are The Bay City Rollers?'

And they'd add things like: 'What a strange name.' Even after I'd got them a few bookings it was still that name that caused trouble. You see, it didn't fit easily across a single column in the newspapers when dance hall promoters wanted to take advertisements. It could prove not only cumbersome, but costly, because one has to pay for advertisements by the line or number of words used.

Anyway, we did start to get a few regular jobs and I agreed that I wouldn't take anything from the group. I said we'd put all the money into a kitty, as long as the boys didn't take any money either. Because that was the only way we could start to buy better equipment. Derek, in particular, was playing drums on some really old equipment and it was obvious that his drums were the first things we should replace.

It was now about the autumn of 1969 and we got another booking at The Top Storey Club. This time, though, it was a Saturday night booking, which really was a very important engagement for us. Saturday nights there were so much more popular than Sundays.

You're probably wondering who was in the group in

those days. Well, there were the Longmuir brothers, of course. There was Nobby Clark and a chap called Dave Pettigrew. He was a very intellectual type and we called him Dave the Rave. Then there were two other brothers – Greg and Mike Ellison.

I realized at the time that The Rollers did need changes, because there were various weaknesses in various parts. But as guys they were all very nice. Greg Ellison wanted to get on at school, and I don't blame him for that. As a matter of fact, I think it was intelligent of him to want to do that. Mike Ellison just didn't fit in at all. He was doing the singing with Nobby and I didn't think there should be two singers. So eventually Mike Ellison left the group.

Of course, today, The Rollers are known not only for their music, but the clothes they wear. At the start, though, they used to wear jeans, denims, that sort of thing with tee shirts. They didn't have any money and I didn't have any money either. So basically they wore blue jeans – except Derek, who wore pink ones. He had dyed a denim jacket pink, which I thought was incredible, and had put this blue frill off the top of some curtains along the back of his jacket. It really looked like something Clint Eastwood might wear – really eye catching. I've always found that about The Rollers: they're a very inventive bunch of young people, so that even when none of us had any money they always looked good. Anyway I decided that we should buy a set of suits to make us look just that little bit better. There wasn't anybody actually phoning me back, saying: 'We have got to have The Bay City Rollers.' It was a matter of sitting at the phone all day during the week and on Saturday afternoons and ringing promoters and halls. We even rang on Sunday nights because you just have to grab these people when they are there.

At that time we were playing locally in and around Edinburgh. We could never get into Glasgow because it was a different type of circuit at the time.

Even after I had started managing them, The Rollers were very much a part-time band because they were still at school. Luckily, they all went to the same school, so they could discuss things during break and at lunchtime. As soon as they came out of school each afternoon one of them would ring me up at home and ask if there had been any more bookings etc. It was an amazing time for all of us. At times it seemed almost unreal.

We did start something then that went on for many years and that is we used to have a picture night. There would be about seven of us and we'd all pile into this old van and drive up the road to the ABC cinema in Lothian Road, Edinburgh. Sometimes we'd go to the Odeon instead. The Rollers have always enjoyed films and so have I.

In fact, even now when we're on tour, or the boys are staying in a hotel, we hire a few films and show them on the wall on our own projector.

When the boys were making their second album they nearly drove me mad with watching Westerns. I think I've now seen nearly every Western ever made. Mind you, they've got a bit choosey these days: they won't watch black and white films anymore. Recently, I was in charge of the projector and wound on a black and white film. As soon as it started, all the boys let out a loud groan, so I tried to kid them into thinking there was something wrong with the projector and that the colour would come on in a few minutes. But after ten minutes they demanded I take it off and put on another film instead. And to think now that in those not so distant days we'd watch anything on our film nights . . .

The boys are certainly the opposite to my mother and

father, who are now in their early seventies. For their Christmas present last year I bought them this huge colour TV which can be controlled from an armchair. But every time I go home I catch my father watching all the programmes on it in black and white. He turns the colour off because they prefer black and white!

When we did eventually get The Rollers' first set of suits, we economized by taking the material to this very kind lady who made the suits for £6 a time. I've still got the receipts. All the suits were pink – an orangey sort of pink, to be accurate, and the boys used to wear white shirts and black bow ties. You can imagine what they looked like.

Still, musically, they had started to improve, and when Mike Ellison left I kept the group down to five – a number we've stuck with ever since. By then, The Top Storey appearances were beginning to build up a bit, and after a while the Craig brothers, who ran it, asked if The Rollers would like to do a residency there.

We were offered the Saturday night. We thought this was sensational and we couldn't believe our luck. We were given a wage rise, too, which meant we were paid £8 for regular appearances. It was at that time that The Rollers started to get really popular locally.

We played to full houses every time, and as a result we were also asked to play at another club in Edinburgh, called The International Club. It is now called The West End Club. The club stayed open until two in the morning and we were asked to play from midnight till closing time, which meant we could go on there after finishing at The Top Storey. It was the beginning of 1970 by now and we were paid £7 for the second gig, so we were earning the grand total of £15 a night, which was quite strange after we'd been used to getting a fiver or so.

We became even more popular in Edinburgh and people were very nice to us, and they lent us vans and carried equipment for us and things like that. By this time the Palais had closed down and I had packed my job in with the company. I was asked to go to Belfast and play, but I preferred to stick with the challenge of this group, The Bay City Rollers. Everyone I met at the time would nod their heads sadly and say the same thing: 'You're wasting your time.'

So I went back to my dad's business in Prestonpans. He ran a wholesale business that had really grown into quite a big business over the years and I went back to that as a lorry driver. It meant I was able to put more time into The Rollers, driving lorries by day and going with them to gigs at night. I decided at the time that I would really have to try very hard to get them work outside Edinburgh, because it was reaching saturation point there. They were becoming successful, but we had to aim for bigger things.

So I phoned up an agent I knew in Glasgow, Ronnie Simpson, and tried to get him interested in The Rollers. He came up with one or two jobs: one was in Hamilton, just south of Glasgow, which was amazing as far as we were concerned because we'd only been used to playing around locally.

By this time there had been some more changes in the line-up as we continued to search for the right format. Out had gone Dave the Rave Pettigrew. In had come Keith Norman. Keith was a really pleasant person. I think he's in the Merchant Navy now. I've never heard from him for years.

Now they were getting even more popular. And when we appeared at the Trocadero, Hamilton, it was quite a riot. Things just seemed to happen. All the kids gathered around and by this time The Rollers had started making themselves much more way out clothes.

They'd made flared trousers out of satin and all that kind of thing, and I think that was the first night we heard a scream during the boys' act. Everyone backstage was very pleased and we were paid a handsome £20, which to us was really big time.

Afterwards, we helped lug the equipment out into the van and then we all piled into the back and drove home to Edinburgh very excited. To actually come over from Edinburgh and conquer a gig near Glasgow meant a lot to us that night. You can imagine we were pretty pleased with ourselves!

I'll confess it was very uncomfortable in the back of that van, hunched up amongst all the equipment, and I decided that I must try and get a small car if we were going to spend more time driving around Scotland. The trouble was the same thing that confronted every decision we had to make: money. Or, to be precise, the lack of it.

I did have a car at the time, but it was very small and it would have been just as uncomfortable for the group as the van. I just had to get a bigger car and the only person I could turn to was my mother. She did eventually lend me the money to get a bigger car, but I later lost it to pay another debt for The Rollers.

Still, when we were booked for a return at the Trocadero, Hamilton, we were able to drive there and back in comfort. We also got more bookings on the West Coast of Scotland around Glasgow. And it was at one of these concerts that we first realized how rough things could be when you played dance halls near Glasgow. We were booked in at the Motherwell Town Hall and I'll always remember that night because we got a right tanking. It was like something out of the Wild West – or one of those Western films the boys are so fond of. Come to think of it, perhaps that's why they're so fond of them – it reminds them of the hard old days.

It was a Friday night dance, as opposed to a concert, which meant everyone had to stand back against the walls to let people dance. Our 'roadies' were standing in front of the stage watching the group when somebody shouted: 'You shouldn't be standing there – get back.' The roadies said they were just doing their job and watching the group, and the next thing somebody attacked one of them and the whole hall started fighting. Eventually The Rollers managed to pull the roadies through a door from the dance floor that led backstage. But they really had to pull. It was like a tug-o-war, because there were as many people the other side trying to drag them back into the dance hall. As soon as we'd got them through, The Rollers barricaded themselves in a backstage room while the crowd tried to rip the door down. To me, it was pretty frightening, but the boys didn't seem all that bothered. I think they were more put out that they hadn't finished their act.

Eventually the police arrived and stopped the trouble and we gingerly pulled away all the furniture from the door and let them in. They got us out in the end all right. In fact, we got a lot of that sort of thing when we were playing that side of the country. It could be quite tough and I've a scar or two to prove it. I've had my nose broken, a few black eyes and I've been kicked about the floor a few times during the gradual rise to fame of The Rollers. Of course, they've always been on stage at the time so they've escaped although even they have had a few near scrapes. They were good too, you know, very handy with their guitars if we were in trouble. If they saw the roadies or myself were in trouble they'd soon come to our aid, swinging their guitars above their heads like clubs!

I don't think the public know quite how rough things are for groups when they're starting out. People tend to judge them from when they're on Top of the Pops and have made it. It's often said that pop singers get their money too easy and are overpaid. I certainly know different – and so do The Rollers. You could say that at one time we were literally fighting our way to the top.

Of course, a lot of these fights start because of jealousy. A bloke takes his girl friend to a dance and then she goes all mad over a guy in the band and this drives the fella mad, so he tries to have a go at the band. It doesn't happen at concerts, because everyone is sitting down, but it can happen quite easily at dance halls, where beer and drinks are on sale. There was a time when I used to worry myself to death going along to some of these dance halls.

But we'd have some really nice things happen as well – like the first time we played in Dundee. As soon as the boys went on everybody started screaming and screaming. It was incredible. The group couldn't believe it. They kept looking behind them to see who was standing at the back of them, because all the kids were screaming and putting their hands up in the air and everything like that. They really went down a storm that night, and yet they thought the audience were yelling for somebody else. I was delighted, and I walked around the balcony area about three times trying to work out why the audience were screaming. Then when they went to get off stage all these girls wanted to rip their clothes. I discovered later that a pop group had never been allowed to play that hall before. Obviously, the youngsters were just ready for a group because they'd always had to dance to a big band. And not only were The Bay City Rollers a group, but they were a young group that their audience could identify with. And that was very important, too.

It was a great morale booster for the group, and I believe it was that Dundee appearance that caused us to take off. It was really a lucky break, and everyone needs one of those at least once in their lifetime.

'KEEP ON DANCING'

There were to be more changes within the group.

The next person to leave was Greg Ellison. As I've said, he really wanted to concentrate on his schoolwork and because of our success we were spending more and more of the boys' spare hours travelling around Scotland.

Greg had also got a girlfriend by then and wanted to spend more time with her. We parted on the best of terms, and I feel that he did a lot for The Rollers and had helped very much in getting them to where they were at that time. He was replaced by Dave Paton, who is now in a group called Pilot.

Now we were beginning to earn between £25 and £30 a night and were collecting quite a bit of equipment. Although we were playing Glasgow, we kept appearing at the Top Storey in Edinburgh, because that, naturally, was one of our favourites. By then we were playing there once every three weeks. I tried to cut down, which sounds daft, doesn't it, after all the time it had taken to get work for the boys? I always had this feeling that we mustn't become just another successful local band. We would be a big national band and in order to do that we must play all over the place, and in as many places where we were unknown as we were known.

There was terrific competition at the time between the groups playing in Scotland. The Beachcombers were still big and there were groups like The Phoenix, The Tandem and The Index. And a lot more clubs were opening up in Edinburgh alone.

Despite all this activity we could hardly make ends meet. Work it out yourself: you don't make money earning an average of £25 three times a week when you've got to pay for the hire of van, and petrol, equipment, roadies and things like that.

The boys had just left school and were starting to get jobs. Derek had taken up an apprenticeship as a joiner at the age of fifteen. He was working by day and travelling at night. So was Alan and so was Nobby.

We were earning just over £60 a week, but I was always having trouble with our books and getting letters demanding that I pay up for such and such a bill within seven days. It was very much a hand to mouth existence – borrowing a bit here, paying off a bit there, and all the time driving the lorry so that I'd have some money coming in to spend on the group. And, of course, when you need things to go right for you, financially, they don't. For example, around this time Alan had seen a Gibson bass guitar which had belonged to a member of a group called The Embers. The Embers had broken up and this guy was selling the guitar, which was very special. Alan had saved up some of his money and I said I'd try to do a deal with the chap to buy it for £80.

I remember meeting Alan on a Saturday morning and him saying to me: 'Do you think you'll manage to get it for that price?' That Saturday Alan helped me out on the lorry delivering to various shops around the Edinburgh district so that I'd get finished early enough to see about the guitar.

When I brought it back, oh, he was dead pleased with it. Really pleased. You see, it was the best thing he'd owned in all his life, and music meant everything to him. It was really worth about £120. By that time we'd also seen another guitar we liked. It was a Les Paul and we put £25 down on it to buy it on the never-never. We believed that the only thing that really mattered now was our sound and these two guitars would make all the difference. Everyone was agreed about that.

Anyway, a week later my mother called me, just as I was setting out in the lorry, to say our roadie was on the phone. I couldn't grasp what he told me at first. He kept our van in the street outside his house and when he'd gone down that morning he'd discovered it had been broken into. Among the stuff missing was the Les Paul guitar and some amplifying equipment. We never ever found any of that stuff again and at the time I really thought the group would have to break up. It was a devastating blow. It not only removed some of our vital and best equipment, but also left us deeper in debt. You see, we had to keep on paying the HP even though we no longer had the guitar. I felt like sitting down and weeping. I didn't know how to break the news to the group. It was really depressing. I was still stunned as I walked out and got into the cab of my lorry. 'What's the matter?' my mother asked. But that was one time I never answered her. I couldn't. I felt so sick. I just drove off on my round. Later, I phoned the boys to tell them.

There is no doubt that the group would have broken up if it had not been for a chap called Pete Seaton, who ran a music shop in Edinburgh. He kindly loaned us two guitars for several months without any payment at all. So, you see, there are still kind people around when you really need them. Pete knew how keen The Rollers were, and he wasn't willing to see them stopped overnight. Those two old guitars saved our lives and are responsible for The Bay City Rollers being around today.

Apart from this, things were still getting worse, financially, and Keith Norman was next to leave. He was replaced by Billy Lyll who is now a member of Pilot.

I never really felt that Keith was that interested. I don't think he was interested in making sacrifices or fighting to get on, which are two qualities you have to have if you are going to stick with a group you believe is going to get to the top. And what's the use of being content in not getting to the top? I didn't have anything against him, but I just felt he was not quite right for a pop group.

As if we didn't have enough trouble, there was another outside influence at work at the time. It was the period of what became known as 'heavy' music. Everyone was trying to see this as the new 'in' thing and here were we playing what is known as teenage music. Well, I've always believed in our type of music. I didn't think 'heavy' music did anything for entertainment, and we just kept on doing what we knew best.

Still, all this meant that I was getting deeper and deeper into debt keeping The Bay City Rollers in business. I had to borrow £100 off my mother and £60 off my brother to help clear some debts. About that time, too, we were really having to pay a lot of money hiring vans. We might get £30 for playing, but a van and a driver was costing nearly £18 and we were paying another £3 in agents' fees, which meant we had to go there and back for £10. And we had to give a pound or two to roadies! So you can see there wasn't much left in it for us. What there was had to be put towards paying off our debts which never seemed to get smaller.

So we decided to buy a van. And then, as everything seemed to be going wrong for us, something went incredibly right. Ronnie Simpson, the man who had first booked us into that Hamilton gig and had since been really pleased with what The Bay City Rollers could do, had been in touch with someone at Bell Records in London.

The head man at Bell at the time was Dick Leahy and he flew up to Scotland to hear a lot of groups.

Dick Leahy meant to visit only Glasgow and then fly back to London. But as luck (ours, that is) would have it, he missed his plane and decided to go to Edinburgh and fly back from there.

The Rollers were playing that night. Dick Leahy, who had actually got to Edinburgh airport with Ronnie Simpson, was told the next plane would not take off for several hours. He asked if there were any clubs open in the city. Ronnie had always referred to The Bay City Rollers jokingly as a 'weenybop' band because heavy rock was the new 'in' thing and that's what he thought Dick Leahy had come to hear. But he still suggested that Mr. Leahy might like to hear us. They both arrived at the Caves Club in Edinburgh with another chap called Tony Calder. The basement club was packed and my knees began to knock with nervousness as I thought to myself: 'Who are all these people up from London to see The Rollers?'

When the group did come on, I think Dick Leahy was knocked over because all the kids started screaming and pushing and pulling and things like that. Leahy couldn't believe it, and Tony Calder said he hadn't seen anything like it for years. That was the start of Dick Leahy really becoming very interested and involved in The Rollers. He had a lot of faith and played quite a main part in the group, although I must admit I had many disagreements with him. Lots of times I felt he never treated me as a manager – rather as a mate, or someone who'd tagged on with them. But, anyway, that was that. Dick Leahy met The Rollers and so did Tony Calder, and they all became very interested.

The Rollers had played for an hour and a half that night and they were still influenced by the Beatles. But they did have their own numbers, too, such as 'Give Me A Little Sign'. Their clothes had changed again by then, too. Their suits had gone; I think they'd worn them off their backs. They were wearing very casual things and stuff that they had made for themselves, like blue satin trousers with white shirts. But I was too busy watching the reactions of Dick Leahy, the big record boss from London, to notice much about the boys' clothes that night. I felt really proud for them. At last something seemed likely to happen, especially when Mr. Leahy asked if he could see them again and started mentioning recording contracts.

That was really the beginning of The Bay City Rollers' recording career. Mr Leahy did come up again later, but Tony Calder had come up before him and had signed a contract for a record production deal. Tony Calder did a deal with Dick Leahy afterwards and later we found out that Bell Records had advanced Calder's production company a sum of money. By this time, though, Calder's production company had gone bankrupt, and we didn't get the advance on our first record. It would have been about £3,000 or £4,000 and we could dearly have done with it because we were so hard up. But that was that – the money had gone. Mr. Leahy then asked us to sign straight to him and introduced us to a producer called Jonathan King.

Mr. Leahy was now coming to Scotland all the time to see us and we were once again getting excited, although, as usual, our money troubles didn't help. We also had to travel down to London once or twice, which cost us money, and by the time Bell records had decided we were signed to their company it seemed to take a hell of a time before a single was coming out. That's when we lost another member of the group – Dave Paton. I think he thought it was all rubbish about our recording contract because it was taking so long to happen. We brought in Neil Henderson who seemed to fit in all right. By then 'Keep On Dancing' had been chosen for our first single, and we all went down to London again and this time met Jonathan King.

Things were very different on those early journeys to London compared to the comfort we travel in today. We set off in this old van, all piled in the back with the equipment once again and headed for London. We drove down the A1 until we reached Newcastle and found a small transport cafe on the side of the road. We call them 'greasy houses', and we were limited to spending thirty pence each because we were that short of money. If you've ever had to buy breakfast or dinner for 30p you'll know what it was like. Anyway, we had got as far as Peterborough and the van broke down. The big end had gone and that was that. It was five in the morning and we were all shivering in the back wrapped around with blankets, and aching from being pushed up against the equipment. We had to get the van towed in, and the guy wanted money as soon as he'd done that. When he told me how much he wanted for mending it I was horrified. We were 80 miles from London and I said I'd pay him later if only he could get us there. This guy was really great. He drove us – and all our gear – all the 80 miles . . . straight to the studios.

We were using Olympic Studios in Barnes, which is very near the Thames just over Hammersmith Bridge, and I must say when we were going across that beautiful bridge I felt we'd never see the studios and that our recording career would be over before it had begun.

We got to the studios at two o'clock, although we weren't due to be there until much later. From the outside there is nothing glamorous about the Olympic Studios: they look a bit like an old cinema, and yet within their walls most of the top recording stars in Britain have recorded over the past years – including Slade, who claim it was the only place they could get an authentic stamping sound in the corridor for one of their hits.

Well, there we were – dumped on the doorstep for the start of our great recording career. We didn't exactly feel like stars and we spent the afternoon wandering around Barnes. There was a coffee place around the corner from the studios, which most of the musicians used, but we were really skint by now and couldn't even afford a cup of coffee. So we went back to the studios ready to set up our equipment. By then Jonathan King had arrived in a big white car, with darkened windows and, believe it or not, a streamlined TV aerial on top.

We were to spend four days recording with him and he was very kind. I think he realized our position, and saw to it that the boys had plenty of coffee and sandwiches, which was a blessing since we were broke. He used an orchestra with violins and things to back us up and one of the tunes we recorded, of course, was 'Keep On Dancing'. I'm sorry to keep on about how little money we had, but when you have been through an experience like we had, it's apt to stay rather firmly in your mind. For example usually groups making records in London stay in smart hotels, as we do now. But that first time in the studios we crept away at night to a hotel which allowed seven of us to sleep in the same room, some on camp beds. We managed to get this room for £3 a night, and on that budget we decided we could have one meal a day to keep us going.

We had quite an argument to keep our hotel bill so low. When I say we had one meal a day I don't mean a three course slap-up job. A 'meal' to us in those days meant a mug of tea and some ham sandwiches. So really it paid us to keep working in the studio because we got free coffee and things there. We didn't like the hotel very much, so we used to go out first thing in the morning and get a good wash and brush up. The boys have always been very keen on keeping clean, and we felt a bit shabby staying where we did. But it was a necessity and everyone realized that, but we never let either Bell Records or Jonathan King know how we were living in London that week.

How different things are today. As I'm remembering this story, staying in a hotel with a swimming pool, and a sauna bath, Woody has just ordered a prawn cocktail and a glass of milk for breakfast on room service. The phone never stops ringing with inquiries and we've got a colour TV in each of our rooms. A film projector, of course, is set up on a table in my room with a pile of movies ready to be shown.

Eventually, when we had finished recording I got a phone call from the garageman in Peterborough to say he had mended the van and would I collect it. I caught the train up there and drove the van back to London to collect the boys and their equipment.

Then we set off back to Scotland in high spirits because the recording had gone well.

The record came out a few weeks later and at first it didn't seem to be taking off in the way everyone thought it would. Of course everyone making their first record truly believes it's going to get to number one. But sometimes a record can take a long time to climb up the charts, and that's what happened in our case.

In fact, it was six months before 'Keep On Dancing' became a success, which is quite amazing. We changed musicians yet again in that period; Billy Lyll was replaced by Archie Marr, who stayed with us only for a short time. All this time I was watching very closely three other groups in Edinburgh in my search for the perfect Bay City Rollers line-up. They were The Tandem, The Index and above all a group called Kip, who soon got the name of being the reserve team for The Rollers. They were perfect for this role because they, too, were very young, and that is what The Rollers are all about.

At that time I tended to pick Rollers on personality rather than musical skill. I always thought that you could take someone who had an image and train them to play; you can have the most fantastic musician but then you'd probably have to spend a fortune on plastic surgery or something like that to get him right as far as image is concerned. Once there was a group in America called The Monkees, who were created. They just picked a group of good-looking guys and made them into hit recording artists and made that TV series with them. But I don't think that could ever have worked with The Bay City Rollers. We were more of a personal type of thing. There has to be a close association between the group and the manager for a start. There has to be a certain amount of apprenticeship served. I always think this period of apprenticeship has to be gone through for a group to be any good. The Beatles certainly did it when they played in Hamburg for quite a time, and The Bay City Rollers have done it as well.

I couldn't go out tomorrow and pick five nice guys and say: 'Right, you're going to be as big as The Rollers.' It just does not happen like that. It's something else that seems to work: it's being skint, being on the road and travelling together. They also have to be interested in playing. They had to be interested in really getting on, and I sort of psycho-analysed them every time I interviewed them for the job.

I look at the group today and I see in Woody the cheeky-faced type of guy. Actually he's got a very nice character. He's a very nice guy. I would say he had that kind of image. He definitely has the 'boy next door' look, I should say. Derek has got the very quiet type image, and he is a very quiet person. I once drove with Derek all the way from Edinburgh to London and I think he said only one thing. When we were nearing Birmingham, he suddenly suggested: 'Do you think we should have something to eat?' He's very nice and all that, and you couldn't meet a nicer guy but he doesn't say much. Alan is an altogether different sort of person, he's a bit of an extrovert, although he doesn't show it much on stage. He sort of shows off, but only in company, and yet when he goes on stage he seems to lose it all as soon as he has a big audience. He has the mature type of looks that appeal to mature young ladies. Eric? Well, he's the moody one. He can be pretty moody at times and he's inclined to be more serious about things. He's very serious about song-writing. He worries a lot. He worries about the group. Bay City Rollers are his life. He's always worried in case they are going to break up, or somebody's going to try and break them up, things like that. He's very interested in song-writing and he'll go away into the country and sit with Woody and write songs for days on end. Then there's Leslie.

People sometimes think that Leslie is a bit full of himself, but he's not really. He's rather a nervous person and I like him very much. I think he will go on to bigger things. He does a lot of talking and likes to be in on things a lot, because he is nervous. He always worries about The Bay City Rollers too. I think he always worries: 'What'll I do if they break up?' . . . 'Am I really a star?' . . . 'How could this have possibly happened to me?' . . . I think he is very grateful for everything that has happened to him, but sometimes people do get the wrong impression; they're inclined to think he is a little bit big-headed. I don't think of him that way at all. He's not big-headed – and neither are any of the others. I don't think they have changed a bit since we slept seven to a room in that London hotel while we made our first hit.

With the time it took to get to the top, I don't think you could get big-headed. We honestly thought we had had it, but we had a marvellous guy called Chris Denning who was doing the promotion of the record and he really fought for it. He wouldn't take 'no' for an answer. The promotion man has a very hard job to do, because it is down to him to persuade disc jockeys, radio and TV producers, all those sorts of people, to play your record. He kept saying to us: 'It's going to be a hit ... We're going to make you a hit,' and he kept chasing everyone to play it on the radio. He believed the group had a good future, and the record took off. But there was a lot of hard work behind it.

Dick Leahy had faith too, but I never really knew with Jonathan King. I often thought he had lost it when the first record didn't get much airplay. But Chris Denning was really in there fighting to the end. Certainly, looking back, I feel there is a lot more Jonathan could have done.

As for the boys, well, they thought they were really into a lot of money once the record got in the top fifty. We just sort of went crazy at the time. Up until then we had been going out for about £35–£40 and about this time an agent travelled up to Scotland to see if he could sign up the group. He represented a London agency and he was called Barry Perkins. Today he is my partner. He had a lot of faith in the group, too, and with the record going into the charts we at last found that we were in demand. We signed with the agency that Barry was working for at the time and suddenly we found ourselves playing in Dundee one night for £40 and Bournemouth way down on the South Coast of England the next.

We went on at midnight in Dundee and played for an hour. After we had packed all the gear in the van it was two o'clock before we could set off for Bournemouth on the longest journey we had ever made together. I'd say it was almost 600 miles from Dundee to Bournemouth.

We went down the M6 and about 5 a.m. we pulled into the services pull-up at Forton, which is just before Manchester. We were really exhausted by now because the boys had only just finished playing and we'd already travelled all this way. But we were driven on by the sensational price we were getting for playing in Bournemouth. It was £125 – or about three or four times the amount we'd ever been paid before.

We couldn't believe it when Barry Perkins told us over the phone and I remember blurting out aloud in front of the group: 'Oh, God, this is it.'

This place at Forton has a place on top that is a big round building and we nicknamed it The Whirly. Even now, when we pass it, all the boys shout out: 'There's The Whirly.' So there we were at five in the morning at The Whirly. A quick breakfast (and for once we could afford bacon and eggs, as well as a mug of tea!) and soon we were back on the road again, refreshed and excited at the thought of playing our first gig in England.

The journey seemed to go very quickly and all the way we were getting more and more excited at the prospect of appearing before a totally new audience.

But then, seven miles outside Bournemouth disaster struck.

The big end on the van had gone again. We were supposed to be at the place at about five o'clock and it was already mid-afternoon. It began to look as if we had driven nearly 600 miles for nothing. Quickly, we hired a van to come out and pick up our gear. We were overcharged a lot for that because the van hire people charged us £20 for taking the gear the remaining seven miles into Bourne-

31

mouth. We had to stay in Bournemouth for three days, which meant that by the time we'd paid for the van, our hotel bill, and got back to Scotland we had actually lost £40 on the whole deal.

In fact, the whole trip was a disaster. We hadn't gone down at all well in Bournemouth. It wasn't our sort of town. We played in a discotheque for over-21s and they just weren't our audience. Really, we would have done better to stay at home in Scotland, except that we had broken into England at last and I felt that if we could get the right dates then we would become a nationwide success. But youth clubs in England were still only paying £40 a night, and that was impossible as far as we were concerned. Eventually we did start getting gigs all over England at £125 a night, but with all that travelling and six people in the group to support, plus the van and equipment we didn't make much money.

So there we were – a record in the Top Ten, and once again no money to call our own. Because we had lost our £4,000 advance on the single to a company that had gone bankrupt it meant we actually owed the record company money advanced to us.

'MANANA'

For me, there was only one thing to do. Even though I was the manager of a top pop group, I decided to go back to work driving the lorry.

At the time we were in the charts, the group were actually working on the lorry with me, as a way of earning more money. They'd be loading and delivering and for one or two members of the group this became too much. Neil Henderson and Archie Marr both left at the same time and were replaced by Eric Faulkner and John Devine. So the line-up now was: Alan Longmuir, Derek Longmuir, Eric Faulkner, Nobby Clark and John Devine. And if you think we'd already been through hard times, the next part of the story may shock you. For it was only now that we began to suffer the worst.

Everyone thinks a record in the charts means the end of a group's worry. Well, often it's only just the beginning. And so it was with The Bay City Rollers.

I realized we were playing the wrong venues. We were being put into cabaret venues before people in their thirties who were all sitting around tables, having a drink. There's nothing wrong with people in their thirties, and there's nothing wrong with having a drink (even though we never touch the stuff) but it was no good for The Rollers at that time. The group was just not getting through to them.

It wasn't long before we were offered our first appearance on Top of the Pops – the one show that all groups would give their right arm to appear on when they're on the way up. I suggested that the group should go for a different image when they did the show, I didn't want them looking the way they were when they appeared on those cabaret dates – in nice suits with big bow ties and striped shirts. But I was advised by various people that they should. In a way I was bulldozed into them appearing like that. So when The Rollers did their first Top of the Pops it was all a bit of a joke, because they'd turned up with these big bow ties and brown suits. They looked like a cabaret band.

It was obvious I was resented as the manager of a group coming all the way from Scotland, which is where we intend to remain. There was never any chance of us moving down to London. They seemed to think I didn't know what I was doing and right at the beginning I must confess that they were right. I would say I was a very stupid person at that time. I've learned now and I won't make the same mistakes. I think I did a lot of foolish things. In the first place I never got any respect because they reckoned I was a bit soft. They reckoned they could walk all over me and trample on me, just because I was a young manager who had come from Scotland and who knew nothing.

Several times people tried to get me out of managing The Rollers. They tried to take over the group themselves but they reckoned without the loyalty within the group. If they'd been through what we'd been through together then they would have known the group would not go with some man in London they hardly knew.

When the initial success of 'Keep On Dancing' started to die out we still kept driving up and down the country doing one night gigs in dance halls and places. We'd had no word from Jonathan King about our next single. I phoned Dick Leahy several times to ask him if he would be bringing out another single and what was happening. This state

34

of affairs seemed to go on and on, with no result at the end of it. It was very frustrating, because the boys had had a winner with their first single and now no one appeared to have a plan of action for us.

Then we heard that Jonathan King didn't have time to go back into the studios and they would be releasing another of the numbers we had recorded at that first recording session at Olympic Studios in Barnes. All these numbers had been rejected at the time 'Keep On Dancing' was released. Still, out came 'We Can Make Music', and I'll say this for Dick Leahy – the head of Bell in Britain – I really don't think he was very happy about that situation.

When it came out I think it had about four airplays on the radio and died the most horrible death. So there we were – one hit and one miss. Obviously Jonathan King wasn't going to produce us again. Still one thing 'Keep On Dancing' had done for us was to get us out of Scotland and we were now slogging all over the country doing every type of hall, from discos to working men's clubs. In fact, in Scotland we were suffering a bit from over-exposure, so I thought: 'All right, we'll go down to England and we'll do these working men's clubs. It'll keep us away from Scotland.'

That was how we broke out to a bigger audience, but it was still not the audience I wanted The Bay City Rollers to be accepted by. We went into all these cabaret clubs and it was incredible. One night we played a working men's club in Sunderland and this guy got up and walked across the stage halfway through the boys' act, stopped them and announced: 'Pies and beans are now on sale at the back of the hall.' When he finished, he told Nobby he had forgotten something and asked if Nobby would be kind enough to announce: 'Peas and vinegar are on sale too.' Absolutely incredible.

After the announcement there was this huge queue that wound its way right up the side of the hall to the back where the pies were on sale. All this time The Rollers had to keep on playing. It was impossible. But you had to put up with that sort of treatment, because if you didn't you wouldn't get paid. And these jobs usually paid about £80 a time.

You can guess from that that our money had begun to drop again since we were out of the charts. For some jobs we still did get £125. Often we'd take two of these working men's clubs in a night so that we could scoop up £160 and then drive back to Edinburgh. But this way of working posed its own particular problems.

It almost resulted in a fight one night after we'd played in a working men's club in Darlington. The people in charge thought that we should play for three hours. When we arrived, we were told: 'You start at seven and go on until half past eight. Then we'll have a break when we can serve refreshments. After that we have a housey-housey session, and you'll start again at nine fifteen and go on until half past ten.'

I told him he must have made a mistake because we didn't play programmes like that, and I reminded him we'd been in the charts. He replied: 'We've never heard of you before.'

After a terrific row, The Rollers played for an hour and then started packing up their equipment. The people wouldn't let us out of the building with the equipment. The same man was there again and he said: 'You Scotsmen are all the same. Well, this time you're not going to get paid.' We left eventually and arrived at the next venue in time. But I have to admit we never did get paid for that job.

Because of the row, we had precious little time to pack

the gear into the van and drive to the next club, so that night all The Rollers had to become roadies and hump out their own equipment and pack it in the van at double the usual speed. I think Eric, who had just joined, wondered what he'd let himself in for. The Rollers aren't the strongest bunch of lads at the best of times – and that equipment weighs quite a bit. Still they managed it – even though they had a few aches and pains the next day.

Actually, that night we hadn't booked into a hotel anywhere, so we had to sleep in the van because we had a gig further south and weren't due back in Scotland until two days later. It certainly hadn't been our day because the North East of England isn't the warmest of places at the best of times – especially in winter. So there we all were, huddled up around the equipment in the back of the van with mattresses and sleeping bags.

When we used to have to sleep in the van Alan was the Roller who always cracked all the jokes and made us laugh. Derek used to sit and say nothing. But generally we just sat there and chatted away usually about what we'd do when the group made it big. That was always in the backs of our minds. And we'd also wrap ourselves in newspapers at that time and we'd joke about what it would be like staying at The Savoy and places like that.

On this particular night we'd parked the van in a lay-by off the A1. I spread out on the front seat and the Rollers would all huddle in the back because they were about half my size. I also felt that if there was any trouble I was right by the doors and could do the speaking. Also because we kept getting very cold I was in charge of switching the engine on and off during the night so that the heater would warm us all up. But keeping the engine running just to keep the heater working was pretty heavy on our petrol allowance so we couldn't have it on many times.

Mind you, sleeping in vans was nothing new to us. We've slept in the back of vans all over Britain, including Hampstead Heath in London. Imagine if we did that today. We'd be murdered as soon as the fans found the van. Naturally we all prefer the comfort of a hotel to the back of a van, but it's good to have done it, and we owe a lot to Alan for keeping us happy in those days. I've never known a bloke who can really keep a group of people content and laughing in such bad conditions.

There's always the hazard of being woken up by the police when you're camped out beside the road fast asleep in an old van. We must have been woken up literally hundreds of times in our journeys criss-crossing Britain. Usually the police presumed that as we were a pop group we had drugs, which, of course, was totally untrue. Once I remember a policeman getting me to slide open the front door of the van as he shone a torch into the back.

He couldn't believe his eyes when he saw all those little bodies fast asleep. 'Aha, what have we here,' he boomed. Then he asked who owned the van and lots of other questions, and he made everyone get up as he searched the van. He really thought he had caught up with something big, but he hadn't . . . although I'll admit we were always being summonsed for driving a van with balding tyres, things wrong with the van, that sort of thing.

A van can just have a tear on one side caused by an over-eager fan and the police can have you for driving a van in a dangerous condition. I've been prosecuted in court for all sorts of things linked to vans. 'Construction and Use', they call it.

When I've appeared before the magistrates they have always said the same sort of thing: 'Well, if you can't afford to keep a van on the road and look after it, then you have to be man enough to take your punishment.' Usually the fine would be ten or fifteen pounds. I never found any of them understanding. It was always the same old British attitude. They could always come up with a better answer. I did find one magistrate, though, who understood what we were about. He didn't think the tear on the side of our van on that occasion was dangerous, and although he admonished us he also let us know that he understood.

But I've always found the police very hard on groups. They've stopped us a lot in the past and searched us for drugs, and we've never ever taken drugs. None of the boys drink either, except Alan, who occasionally has a lager. Don't forget that when the Rollers started, they were very, very young so that they were not legally allowed to drink in public places. I don't mind anybody having a drink. Just because I don't choose to drink, it doesn't mean that I would stop The Rollers from drinking. But I think I can show them an example by not drinking.

People have accused me of being a Svengali figure looming over The Rollers. I disagree. The Bay City Rollers are really quite free. I only try to show them an example. If any of them wants to drink, it's perfectly OK with me, as long as they never drink on a recording session, or go on stage all boozed up. But when they go back to Edinburgh – off-duty as it were – they can do whatever they like. One paper did describe me as a Svengali but I think The Rollers are young gentlemen; they've all got minds of their own, and they know what's good for them.

They come to me with their problems because I'm older than they are. A lot of people wonder if The Rollers have woman trouble, for example. Well, none of the guys in the group now have had, but Nobby Clark did. He told me he really liked this girl and couldn't give enough attention to her. He asked me if he should leave the group for her, or stay and maybe lose her. I suggested that he should leave the group. Which is what he eventually did.

That was a hard decision for me because he had been the lead singer for a long time. But he had been honest with me and I could only give him an honest answer. He was obviously very much in love with this girl, and if you're going to be in a successful group then you have to realize that your life is never really your own. You get the pleasures, of course, of being a success, but there are a lot of drawbacks. You must often meet people when you would prefer to be lying in bed. You must always look your best and remember that people are always looking at you critically and closely. Your time is hardly ever your own.

After the failure of 'We Can Make Music' things began to get really tough again. I was working as hard as ever on the lorry, and when we weren't playing at the weekends Eric would come out on the lorry with me with John Devine. Alan and Derek were doing odd jobs around the place, and strangely enough at the time one of our biggest difficulties was finding somewhere to practise. So we decided to build our own little studio. We set off looking for premises. As I was driving around in the lorry I would keep a look out and often Eric would say, 'There's a place'. We'd stop and look, but it never seemed the sort of place we were searching for.

In the end, we found the right place staring us in the face at my dad's store. It was the back of the garage. There was an old room there that had never been used, and we built it up into a nice little studio over the months. We used lots of cheap things to make the studio, so that it wouldn't cost very much. You read of all these big groups buying their own studio to be built at home for £40,000. Well, ours was a very different place altogether. For sound-proofing, the boys shovelled up sand from the beach and Alan and Derek did all the joinery work. In the end it was beautifully sound-proofed. It's actually in a sand bunker now, and the group still sometimes practises there.

We had a great time building it. It was a laugh all the time with Alan, as usual, leading the way. They'd had this hit, you see, so they weren't too dispirited by having a failure just afterwards. So there was this group that had got to Number Nine, appeared on Top of the Pops and everything, five or six months later down on the beach gathering up sand and trying to build their own studio.

Now we were really skint and we took any sort of work to get a little money together. We'd do social clubs, drinking clubs, any kind of place. But we were still going into debt, unfortunately, and the debt was growing, really growing.

We were still paying for the van, which had cost us about £1,500. We were still paying out the HP on that Les Paul guitar that had been stolen from our first van all that time ago – and another guitar we had bought for Alan. We had also decided we should take a wage by that time and we started on the grand figure of £6 a week. That's what we were earning while 'Keep On Dancing' was in the charts. You know, when everybody thought we were making a fortune and things were really big we were only taking £6 a week out of the kitty. And by then the National Insurance stamp people were after us as well. They were knocking at the door trying to figure out why we hadn't paid our insurance stamps, because the boys were doing casual work by that time. They kept going up to Derek's house, and then they'd come down to my house because boys who had left the group had told them: 'Oh our stamps were being paid for us.' Actually we hadn't been paying stamps because we couldn't afford them.

All this time I never told my mother how hard up we really were. I'd borrowed money from her in the past, but usually managed to pay it back. I didn't want her to know just how really bad things now were. But one day a man came and said he was going to take the van away. I had to tell her because she was pretty worried when she overheard what was going on. So once again my mother came to our rescue and gave me the money so we could keep the van.

I'd spent a lot of money by this time on publicity. Many people might think this was stupid, considering the position we were in, but I felt it was an essential.

I thought we should be handing out photographs of the group and I'd also sent pictures of the group to every disc jockey at the BBC. At one time I was sending them one photo a week. I kept sending everyone who worked on *The New Musical Express* a photograph of the boys. I thought that was a big paper at the time. Then I sent pictures to all the magazines. This cost us a lot of money. At one time I got a bill from the printers for almost £480, covering posters and photographs. I asked the record company if they could help me, but they said it wasn't their job. So there were a lot of things like that, and it all mounted up, and we weren't earning the big money anymore. Naturally, I tried to keep the worries from The Rollers themselves. They liked handing out pictures of themselves and I couldn't have gone to them and admitted: 'They've cost us £400.'

We'd also started a fan club by this time, which I ran and by the time 'Keep On Dancing' had made it there were about 2,000 members. It's funny to look back at those days, really, because today our postbag alone is around 11,000 letters a day. The fan club now is still run by me but my mother helps and we have other people in as well. Anyway even when we only had 2,000 members I sent them all photographs and news about The Rollers.

It was all weird because on the one hand the group were

incredibly popular and on the other they had no money at all.

Wherever we appeared in Scotland there would be fantastic scenes. Then we'd drive over the border to Birmingham, say, and nobody was interested. We just didn't seem to be getting anywhere. Then, suddenly, we changed record producers. It seemed obvious to me that Jonathan King didn't want to know anything about us. Actually, when I met Jonathan recently he apologized to me and said he felt sorry that he had not spent more time on the group. He also said he was glad we had made it. Anyway, Bell Records got us another set of producers, Ken Howard and Alan Blaikely, who had produced groups in the past like Dave Dee, Dozy, Beaky, Mick and Tich and The Honeycombs and we got excited again. The Rollers were hopeful again, and Howard and Blaikely really believed that this was going to be the beginning of the big thing.

It was now the late summer of 1972 and Ken and Alan wrote a number called 'Manana', which we liked, and off we all went to London again. It was our third single and we all felt it had to be a hit or we could be finished. We thought Dick Leahy at Bell Records would say enough was enough and let us go.

This time the recording was very simple and quick and in no time at all we were back on the road, although we weren't told when the record was going to be released. In fact, it came out in September, 1972, and we heard from Radio Luxembourg that it had been chosen as one of the entries for the International Song Contest in Luxembourg. We were delighted about that because the show was going to be televised all over Europe and Israel and any other place that wanted to take it.

It was really exciting to us because none of us had ever been abroad before, and here were The Bay City Rollers actually invited to take part in a music contest on the continent. It made us feel we were going to become internationally famous.

Next came the problem of how we were going to get there. We obviously could not afford to fly all the way from Scotland, so we decided to drive there in a big old car I'd got at the time. It was a Viscount, and we all piled into that one morning with great excitement and set off for our big adventure. It reminded us very much of setting off for that first gig in England at Bournemouth.

But now we were going international. The Bay City Rollers were going into Europe.

Everything went smoothly as we motored down the M6. We were all in high spirits: Alan had a new store of jokes, Eric was very chatty – and even Derek had a few more things to say than usual. And then it happened.

It's a moment The Rollers and I will never forget. We were just at the end of the M1 with all those hundreds of miles behind us when the steering wheel wrenched violently in my hands. It was as if the car was trying to drive me. We were doing around 70 m.p.h. at the time and I clutched the wheel as tight as I could. Suddenly the car swung violently to the left. I was terrified it was all going to end for us. The car veered from the outside lane to the inside one . . . and then it began to tear off the road altogether. I'd managed to slow it down, but I could do nothing about the steering. Eventually it came to a stop on a high grass bank.

I just sat there shuddering at what might have been. The boys were silent. Slowly, we unwound and opened the doors and got out. We discovered the front nearside wheel had come off and was now still rolling down the motorway in front of us. It was obviously the end of this car – for this journey at least.

44

Then, like a Good Angel the very next vehicle along was a white police Landrover. For once it seemed the authorities felt sorry for us. We told them who the boys were, where we were going and where we had come from and they arranged for a garage to tow the car away. They also tried to get a van to transport the rest of us into London. When they couldn't, they kindly gave us a lift to where the Tube began. That's how we finally got to London Airport. We wondered aloud at the time how the other competitors were getting to Luxembourg. One thing was certain: they wouldn't be going through what we were.

Fortunately, we had only our guitars with us because we were to mime in the competition and Derek could borrow a drum kit. And the car? That was the last I ever saw of that old Viscount. The truth was that after the garageman had towed it away he parked it in his garage and three months later sent me a bill for £300 for parking space! He said it would also cost £300 to put the car right, so I said quite politely down the phone: 'Well, could you just keep the car please.' And that was the end of that.

No, we didn't seem to be very lucky with our transport; because we didn't have much money we had to do things on the cheap and these cheap vehicles were just not up to the mileage we demanded from them.

We eventually arrived in Luxembourg with £12 between us. Luckily, the hotel – and breakfast – was paid for by the organisers. I don't think that hotel had ever seen so many rolls and butter eaten at breakfast before. We just kept eating and eating, knowing it would be our only meal of the day.

As for the song contest, we couldn't have hoped for a better result. We won!

Of course, nothing could hold us down now. Here we were with our new single 'Manana' and having just won a song contest with it. Surely this was the hit we had been waiting for. That is how we felt as we flew back into London Airport. And I must make one small confession on Alan's behalf involving that Luxembourg victory. Afterwards, we were each given a bottle of champagne, so Alan thought he'd see what it tasted like. I don't think he felt too well the next day and as far as I know none of us have drunk champagne since, although if I were to have a drink of anything, champagne is the drink I'd choose.

The strange thing was that despite all this success the record never took off in Britain, although it became quite a hit around the continent and in Israel.

It began to dawn on us that the record was not going to make it in Britain, and that is really how The Bay City Rollers' first holiday came about.

(The Tam Paton story continued on page 91.)

Introducing the Boys

LESLIE

I always wanted to be singer in a group and somebody told me there was this guy called Tam Paton in Prestonpans. They gave me this phone number. So I phoned him up and said that I'd been playing in a group for years and things like that and he asked me to go down and see him. Well I jumped on the next bus and went to Prestonpans.

I actually imagined him to be a fat person with a big cigar, a businessman, or how I thought of a businessman in the music business. But he wasn't. He was really nice. He asked me a lot of questions, but I knew that he knew that I'd been lying about being in a group, because he asked me all sorts of things like what sort of P.A. system did we have? And I said, 'Oh, we've got this and we've got that.' And he asked what the name of the group was and I was giving him different names every time.

I had in fact bought myself a P.A. for £300 and because of this I was in debt and had to take a job in a paper mill outside Edinburgh. I had a scooter at the time so I used to travel up there all the time, and I was on shifts so that meant that I couldn't play in the group some nights. It's funny but at the paper works although I just used to make the tea and see that the paper didn't break on the machine I always knew that I wasn't going to be ordinary. I don't know if everybody gets dreams. But even before I met and knew Tam, I used to have dreams of being up on stage with The Rollers. And when I eventually joined them it was as if I'd been there before.

Tam suggested that I went up to Eric's for guitar lessons. One Saturday when I was there I got a phone call from Tam. He said: 'Is that you, Leslie? How would you like to sing with The Bay City Rollers?' I just about fainted and said 'Aye' and then he added, 'Well, you're singing with them tonight at such and such a gig.'

The only thing that worried me then was how I was going to learn the numbers that they played. Eric started there and then practising with me.

When we arrived at the gig we just had to stick bits of paper everywhere with the words on them. I wasn't so nervous on the first gig because I had to think about reading the words off right and we were on stage. But the next night we were playing in a place where the stage was only about a foot high and we were away from home. It was really packed, and everybody was so close to me, and they were all watching, and suddenly I got really scared. I just started looking away into nothing and trying to concentrate. But I soon picked up confidence. I think the group treated me a bit suspiciously at first, although they were very nice to me. I'm sure none of The Rollers know me fully nor I them.

Maybe in a couple of years I shall.

As for the future I haven't really made up my mind. When I was at school I was very badly behaved and I got the belt all the time. I was expelled and everything and the careers master used to come to me and ask me what I wanted to do when I left school. And all the others used to say things like: 'I want to be a bus conductor.' I couldn't make up my mind what I wanted to do so I just left school without knowing. But I had these dreams and I kept thinking that I was going to be a star, and really I made all haste to get involved in the music business.

The only time I thought that I might not succeed was

on the second night with The Rollers, because I felt I had embarrassed them. I'm awfully conscious of what people think of me and it matters a lot to me, and I've got a bad conscience as well. If I ever do something I'm always saying: 'Oh, I wonder if that's all right,' although I've got a right cocky nature.

So when I think of the future I'm not quite sure. I'd like to go into films, but I don't know if that's what I ought to do. I'd never do anything outside The Rollers. But Tam is going to have another group; and Eric and Woody are writing songs. I don't know whether I'd be a good actor but I also see myself as a racing driver, because I like driving very much.

In December I bought myself a Ford Mustang, which is electric blue and has wide wheels. It can do 160 m.p.h. and it's also very comfortable. In fact I'm the only one in the group at the moment with my own car. I'd love to drive it around wherever we go but that's not possible, and my own car is one of the things I miss most when we're away from Edinburgh.

My nature is that I'll scrimp and scrape over small things, like shampoo and things like that, or always save money on electricity bills and phone bills and things, but when it comes to buying something that I want I'll just splash out a lot of money. I just saw this car and I fell in love with it, and I didn't care how much it cost – and if it was £20,000 I would have bought it.

In fact it was £2,500. It was only a year old and I got it pretty cheap considering that when they're new they're about £6,000.

I'd like to buy a Corvette Stingray. But I'm trying to look at things from a different point of view now because I'm never home to drive it anyway, and I'm paying nearly

£1,000 for insurance on the Mustang so I might even go back to my wee Mini and see what happens.

I'd like to buy a Bentley, maybe, as well. I've seen a Bentley that I liked. They're all different because I like sports cars, sporty type cars, but I like limousines as well. I like sitting in the back of the big Daimlers we hire. It makes you feel really posh.

One year I'd like to enter the Monte Carlo Rally. I've always been in love with mechanical things. If I didn't like something at school I didn't bother with it, so as I didn't like my maths teacher I didn't bother with maths. English didn't interest me either. But I liked my crafts teacher and so I liked handicrafts. I like working with my hands. I've done a lot of busts of people. They're all back in Edinburgh at home.

I've made busts of all sorts of people – including, as a matter of fact, Napoleon. I've had some of that work shown at the Scottish Academy when they had work from all the different schools in the area. And there was a time in my life when I thought I might like to be a potter. I still like playing about with clay and I'd like to do more of that for a pastime, so I think I may well buy myself a kickwheel and some clay.

The trouble is that at present we don't get much time to ourselves. In fact at the moment while we're making our second album and the new single I'm finding the pressures really bad, because we're recording from mid-day until six the next morning, then getting up again and just plodding on.

We've been away from home now near enough four weeks. Even one day at home is good for you, because it seems to settle you. The pressures do affect you. You can do a vocal track in an hour when you first go into the recording studio, but it'll take maybe four hours to do the same thing towards the end of your time. The stress is not so much physical as mental.

Of course, being in a successful group means you have to make sacrifices. It hasn't affected my life that much because I was always a loner anyway. Not because nobody liked me, but because I chose things to be that way. I had my scooter and I had some friends I could see when I wanted to see them: I used to like driving for miles and miles on my scooter. I used to go out in the rain and snow and get soaking wet and I thought that was great. I still like to go away and be by myself sometimes, get some peace, and just sit and think about nothing. When I go home I'll often take the car and go right up to the North of Scotland. I used to go there on my scooter. I would think it's about a four-hour drive. I used to camp up there and just lie around. In summer there was a big pool where you could swim. It was great.

I also used to go hitch-hiking about four years ago, with a mate I had then. I still see this guy sometimes because he pals about with my brother. Once we went hitch-hiking in France. We had £20 between us and we were starving. We were eating apples off the trees and grass and everything, and we slept out in the open in our sleeping bags. My dad's a tailor and he'd made them for us. He'd made these huge plastic bags to put the sleeping bags in so that they kept dry but they used to cause such condensation inside from the heat of our bodies that it used to be wetter inside than out.

I think that's why I'd like to have my car with me when we're on tour because sometimes I could just drive off and be alone for an hour or two. It's not that I like being alone all the time, I don't. In fact, I like being with other people, but it's just nice to get away sometimes.

But then I'm also what you'd call a bit of a family man.

52

I'm very close to my mother and father, and the rest of my family.

My mother still doesn't understand quite what has happaned to me. She says: 'Why don't you go into Opportunity Knocks?' and things like that. She doesn't see me like other people see me. And she doesn't see The Rollers as other people see them either. She sees me as her wee son, and she is still trying to help me which is nice. I'm buying them a big house up in Scotland so that we can all stay together, because I wouldn't want to leave them until I'm a bit older.

I really enjoy going home and I enjoy my mother's cooking. I even cook something when I'm at home, not complicated things, but potato soup. You boil the pototoes and put a ham shank in it and carrots and some chicken stock. It's really nice. Mother makes it better than me, but that's my favourite dish, I suppose. It's really good when it's made right. She makes Irish stew as well. And I like Stovies, we call them Beef Stovies, or sausages, good and spicy. I really like home cooking. I don't like hotel food at all really. I just eat it because I have to eat it when I'm hungry. I used to starve sometimes when I first joined the group because I didn't like the food. And the others used to say that I was a fussy spoilt wee brat. But I like eating tasty food rather than just eating anything for eating's sake.

Let's see what else I'm interested in besides cars, home cooking and music. Well, I'm very interested in people. I feel mainly at ease with Tam as far as being with the group is concerned, because he never annoys me or anything like that, and never fidgets, which is something that really does annoy me. Some people fidget, and like the light on when they're asleep which is one thing that really irritates me. Sometimes I'm very frank with people. You get people who think they're clever and boss you around. I've said to people like that, 'I think you've had a bit too much to drink, why don't you go home?' I'm frank like that, I'm known for coming out with what other people might just think. Some people think I'm cheeky but if I'm with the group and don't like being somewhere, at a party or something like that, I'll just say: 'I don't like being here, so I'd better go.'

If I'm somewhere I don't want to be, it really depresses me and I have to leave. That's why I'd like to have my own car with me. It would sort of relieve me and I wouldn't feel tied down.

What I dislike most is having my photograph taken because it can take so long and I end up bored. You find it hard to smile then and that's when it gets plastic.

I suppose I could be nice to everyone. It's just that if I don't like somebody I let them know. I prefer being nice to everybody and smiling but it does happen once or twice you meet someone who is really horrible.

Still, I do like finding out about people. I like to analyse people. And if I was asked to analyse our appeal, not being bigheaded or anything, but I think everybody in the group is good looking.

We're pretty nice guys and I think that is what appeals to girls somebody who is nice looking and good natured and is doing something better than the guy next door.

Some of the guys might slag us off if they're with their girls and it's all to do with sex, I suppose. It's back to the roots. Not that everybody in the audience wants to have sex with anyone else. But I think if somebody is nice looking then somebody wants to kiss you.

I think all our fans are really nice. A bit possessive sometimes, but they're all really nice. Our audience does not go into a place to smash up seats and things, like the fans of some groups I won't mention.

I get a terrific buzz out of making people happy. Like when I go home if I buy my mother something it makes her really happy and then I feel the same way. It doesn't matter how much it costs as long as she is happy.

When I had no money at all I used to sometimes buy her cigarettes or chocolates, and that used to make her just as happy as anything I might buy today that costs a lot more.

And making people happy is the great thing about being with The Bay City Rollers.

DEREK

It was really the Beatles who drew me into pop.

I remember when I was about thirteen, The Beatles were really big. I went up the ABC in Edinburgh and there were crowds of people on the street and The Beatles already playing inside the cinema. There were police outside and everything. I was really knocked out with all this.

Everybody was screaming. And that's what really gave me the inspiration to start a group because I suppose I thought: 'I'd like to be like that.'

Alan and myself started this group. My cousin was in it as well – to start with it was just a trio. Then we got various guys to play with us and my father bought me a small drum kit. It cost about £60.

We didn't have much money at home but we paid it off on the H.P., and every day we all used to practise in our front room. We were still at school. I'd just started secondary school and some of the guys got fed up pretty quickly. My cousin felt a bit grown up compared with us, so he left.

The first gig we ever got was in a youth club. Memorial Church it was called. That was before we met Tam or anything like that.

There was a group that had a residency there, but their guitarist took ill one Friday night and we were asked to step in. From then on we played every Friday night. It was really good because the people who went there were all our schoolfriends, so we got a lot of support.

I'm telling you this because a lot of people wonder how to start out in pop.

That was every Friday night. I'd never really meant to be a drummer but when we first started the group everyone had chipped in about what they wanted to be. You know the sort of thing: 'Well, I'll be the bass guitarist,' et cetera. And I got left with the drums. Anyway, I've always liked the drums. Then when I joined the Boy's Brigade they taught us how to play them.

You got the choice of whether you played the bagpipes or side drum. I said I'd take the side drum, and I started learning every week. It was military style drumming, not any pop stuff, and that's really how I started to get interested in drums and learn all about them.

We used to play on a wooden table. There might be eight guys around the table plus the leader at the top. He took us through all the rudimentary things. You start with 'Scotland The Brave'. I think that's probably what everyone learns in Scotland if they're learning that style of drumming. You just rat-tat-tat away at the table with your sticks until you're actually good enough to go on parade with a real drum.

I took part in this great march through Edinburgh, just before I got fed up and left the Boy's Brigade. We marched right up Princes Street, the main street in Edinburgh. There I was beating away at my drum. I really felt great because the traffic all got stopped and there was every Boy's Brigade company from Edinburgh marching to the sound of the massed pipes and drums. It can be very moving and make you feel very proud.

To tell you the truth, it didn't really matter if you stopped playing for a while because there were about a hundred drummers and no-one would know the difference if you didn't keep on all the time. I really enjoyed it, and I think it is a good training for any musician.

There's nothing like learning the basics in any trade. I did just the same when I became a joiner after leaving school. At least I got a good training in music and wood-work.

But all that seems a long time ago. So I'll answer a few of the questions we seem to get asked a lot today.

A lot of people ask, what I would put the appeal of The Bay City Rollers down to.

I think it's that the group is young. The people who follow us are like the group, the same age, there's more communication between us and them than, for example, Gary Glitter. Now Gary is a great guy and we've met him several times but he is about 35 years old or whatever he is, and young kids of 14 and 15 cannot really communicate. Then there's the fact that he wears glittery suits which cost thousands of pounds. Kids cannot go out and buy things like that. But they can communicate with us because they can also go out and buy what we wear, and they'll cost just what they cost us. Things like tartan scarves, short trousers.

At the last concert we played 95 per cent of the people came dressed up the same as us, striped socks and all. Well those striped socks cost about 40p, and that goes for most of the things we wear. We don't wear anything that is ridi-culously expensive.

The majority of the people who follow us are girls, al-though we've got a lot of boy fans now. There's a lot of new generation guys 13, 14, 15, 16 . . . those ages. Most of the pop people who are in the business now are older, they're all in their late 20s or early 30s.

Our fans are highly ingenious in the way that they try to get to meet us. On some of the gigs we play at they'll dress up as usherettes in the theatres, maybe they have a pal who is an usherette and they get the uniforms and all off them. It's amazing. Then in the hotels where we stay girls have dressed up as chambermaids and tried to get into our rooms on the pretext of wanting to clean them.

Or they knock on the door and say they're room service and have got a pot of tea for us. We always have security men guarding us nowadays to stop people getting backstage, or into our hotel rooms but it's incredible that there are still one or two girls who always manage to trick their way through even the strictest security. They kid on they're from the newspapers, anything.

The parents are sometimes as funny as the kids. At one time this parent came to see us with a girl who was really hysterical, and she was outside the door pleading with the security men to be let in. She said that she was a Woody fan. She just wanted to see Woody and then she'd be O.K. She was really in hysterics. Really shaking. She was crying and everything, and her mother came to Tam and asked if we could meet the daughter. Tam explained that that wouldn't make things any better, in fact it could make it a lot worse. Anyway, it was decided to let her meet Woody, and Woody comes though the door and this girl just grabbed his hand and the mother's going 'oooohhh,' and the girl started to go all funny and we couldn't explain to the mother about it at all, because we knew this was what would happen. Mothers don't realize what it's like. They can't believe that even when their daughter is all calm and everything and she is introduced to the group she's likely to start crying and maybe go hysterical. We don't know why it happens but it nearly always does.

I've thought about it a lot and I really haven't worked out why they get into such a state. For example, once when we were appearing in Ireland the manager's friend's daughter, or someone like that, wanted to present a teddy bear to the group. Normally we never allow this sort of thing because we know how it'll end up. But she's a nice girl and comes from a good family and suddenly she does the same thing as every other girl has done. She cracked up as well. She comes into the dressing room with the teddy bear, is about to present it to one of us when she cracks and starts to go hysterical. Her mother couldn't believe her eyes. She said: 'She's never been like this before.' It's very odd.

Of course we enjoy it, and I think it's all fun to the fans. Even when they get a bruised leg or something, they've still had the greatest night of their life. For example, Tam's niece went to see The Osmonds in Glasgow and she got a twisted arm or something and came back and said it was the best night she'd ever had! I mean it's good fun, why should anybody knock fun? If they're enjoying themselves, well, that is that.

On the other hand, the pressures of success do have their drawbacks to us personally. I suppose you can't have your cake and eat it. I have to sacrifice quite a lot of things like walking down to the shops when I'm home, which is a thing I've always enjoyed doing. Once we did try to get out. It was when we were in London and we wanted to go to the cinema in Leicester Square and we nearly got hanged. It was just before the time that we'd decided to have our own projector in our hotel, so that we could see any film we want to see.

We'd looked up in the paper and seen this film we wanted to see was on in the West End. We hadn't been to Leicester Square for a long time, this was about the end of 1974, so we drove up in this car and just from nowhere about a hundred girls appeared and started screaming. I think when one girl starts screaming, they all start screaming.

We had to make a quick getaway. A policeman helped us back into the car and we just had to shoot off. These sort of incidents make it impossible to do anything alone. So Bell Records bought us a film projector and we just order up the films we want to see, and play them on the wall in our hotel, wherever we are staying. I like detective and adventure films the best.

So you can see there are pressures in being successful, although don't get me wrong, it's great being successful, especially after the battle we've had.

I've said how we can't go out anywhere. Well, another pressure has affected our off-duty days in Edinburgh. We've actually got to move house because of the fans. It was murder last Christmas when every paper in Scotland announced that The Rollers would be spending the holiday in Edinburgh. I live at home and they took the handle off the front door, unscrewed it. Then they took the nameplate off and they were going to remove the letterbox as well when the police arrived.

The police are really good people in my area of Edinburgh. They were coming up several times a day just to make sure nothing too drastic was happening.

It can be really odd. You peep out and the street seems quiet. You think you'll go out for a few hours, and you just step outside the front door when the girls suddenly come for you from nowhere.

They hide up the stairs of the flats, behind cars in the street, anywhere. It began to get on the neighbours' nerves a bit as well, because the girls started writing on the walls. Where I come from it's easy access for anyone so I'm trying to get a house on the outskirts, a quieter district where no-one will really know me.

The trouble is that once about five girls know where you live they go away and brag to their pals and say, 'Oh

I know where he lives. I've seen him,' and then they tel'
their pals. At one time we had 200 girls outside the house
That day the group were actually leaving from my house
We usually leave from my place if we're setting off to g
somewhere. That afternoon we couldn't get out. Someon
just had to go to the police and ask them to help us. An
all these girls were knocking on the windows and climbin
through the gardens, and trying to get into the house.

I've got a border collie called Jamie who doesn't lik
strangers. He goes off his head, barking all the time, an
that gets on the neighbours' nerves as well. They thin
that if we went out and talked to these girls then every
thing would be all right, but we know it would be 10
times worse. People don't understand.

Not that we don't like our fans, we certainly do, an
we're always down the fan club when we're in Edinburgh
We read a lot of the letters. But even there things are get
ting out of hand because by Christmas time there wer
11,000 letters a day, and you'd really need a volunteer staf
of 50 people to clear them all. It wouldn't pay for itself
We had it at about 25p a year and we lost £3,000 on i
last year. So we had to put it up to 35p, but to pay for it
self it would need to be 75p.

But we do try to keep it as low as possible, and Tam's
mother and father look after it, so the overheads are kep
right down, and we get quite a few people in to help.

We get some funny letters. Some of them would mak
your hair stand on end!

People ask if I have a girlfriend. The truth is that i
would be impossible to have a steady girlfriend at thi
stage. We're always on the move, and if you started takin
girls with you everywhere you went it would be impos
sible. It would be a hassle in itself, and it wouldn't be fai
to the girl either.

You never really get time to think if you miss having a girlfriend, to be quite honest, because there's always something about to happen, like recording the next single and album, getting ready to go on tour, doing photo sessions, interviews, radio and TV shows. You do sometimes say to yourself: 'Oh, I wish I could have about three days off to rest,' and all that, but when you do rest you start to get bored after about the third day. When you get busy, then that becomes a way of life to you. I think it's a good thing that your mind is occupied all the time.

When I'm in a hotel I read quite a lot. I read drum magazines. They wouldn't be of interest to anyone else but they are to me because I like to know about technique and see what other drummers are doing. Then I like buying magazines with film reviews in them. I never ever get into reading books, I've not got the patience to sit down and read a whole book. I've never read many books in my life at all, just short things, magazines and that.

The future of the group? We've been going six or seven years now and in the past there has always been a clash of personalities in the group which has ended up in somebody leaving. As the group is now there are no personality clashes, everybody thinks on the same lines. I think that that means the group will stay together much longer. Obviously we have small disagreements about things, but never serious arguments.

Everybody's sort of friends, like I don't have any close friends outside the group, my friends are in the group.

I think the time this was really brought home to me was when I was rushed to hospital in April of 1974. I've always suffered from asthma and this time I just couldn't breathe. Luckily my sister was in the house at the time. I have an inhaler thing but it wasn't working. My sister went and phoned up Tam and he came up in the car. She had al-

63

ready phoned a doctor but he was taking ages to come. I was starting to panic. It affects your breath even more when you panic, so it was a vicious circle. You're meant to remain calm and then things might get better, but you can't remain calm when you're struggling for your breath.

The ambulance came and I was taken to hospital. As I say, it was then that I realized how close we all were. We were due to play that night, in fact we had lots of dates. The others didn't want to go without me, but we couldn't pull out of dates at the last moment like that, so Jake, our roadie, went on for me.

I was thankful to be in hospital. It did occur to me that I might die when my chest was tightening up and I know it can kill you if you don't get attention. In the hospital they gave me two jabs, one to calm me down and the other which opens your breathing tubes. Anyway I had to stay in hospital for a week and then I wasn't allowed to start with the group for another week and a half.

I was in a public ward and I prefer that to being shut away on your own. I got to know all the nurses and sisters. It was at the time that 'Shang-A-Lang' was in the charts. It was at number two when I was in hospital and everyone knew about it. There was a load of girls trying to get into the ward. They'd borrowed these white coats the radiographers wear and just walked into the ward pretending that they worked at the hospital. Then there were some others who dressed up as cleaning ladies and pretended to be cleaning the ward until they came to my bed when they tried to leap on me.

The sisters in charge of the ward were very understanding, and so were the doctors. A lot of girls would ring up and try to speak to me on the phone saying that they were my sister or some other relative.

People wondered why I didn't go into a private ward.

Well, I don't believe in it. I don't think of myself as being better than anybody else. I mean we've all been brought up rough, nobody's had posh homes, everybody's been brought up like working class people. Just because we've got a wee bit more money than anybody else doesn't mean to say that we're better than them. I was quite happy in a public ward. You can talk to people, and with most of the people being older, it didn't matter to them that I was in a group.

As a matter of fact when I started to get better I took the meals round the ward just like anyone else. It was good fun because it kept me busy. You do get bored in hospital after a while. At first I found one or two things quite embarrassing, like the bedpans. I wanted to go to the toilet shortly after I arrived and I asked where the lavatory was and this nurse says I wasn't to get out of bed and she'd fetch something for me. I was so embarrassed nothing happened for about half an hour. Then she says: 'When you come in here you leave your pride at the door,' and everything was all right. It's just that I'm embarrassed by things like that.

Getting used to the hours they work in hospitals was really weird. You get lights out at half past ten at night, you get wakened at six, and your breakfast comes at seven. It's completely different from the life we live as pop stars. We live completely the opposite hours because we're working till late every night. We're quite likely to go to bed at four or five in the morning if we're recording. Then we get up later as a result.

Hospitals can be quite dramatic places, which is why I suppose they've often been the setting for TV series or films. The time I spent in hospital was no exception.

One night this old bloke who wasn't at all well lifted a lemonade bottle above his head and was shouting at this nurse: 'I'm going to kill you.' And it was obvious that he was going to hit this nurse over the head with the bottle so I leapt out of bed to go and help her. I had to grab his hands and then he was going to hit me over the head with the bottle. I nearly died just at the thought of what might happen and then the night doctors came in and just took him over. When I look back at it it's quite a funny experience. He was annoyed at me because he was shouting, 'I thought you were my friend.' In the morning he couldn't remember a thing about it.

Anyway, I got better, and soon I was back with the group again. But they had visited me, and so had Tam, and I realized how I missed them not only through being in the group, but because they are my friends as well.

People wonder a lot, I suppose, about the money we earn. Well, I've got a great deal with an insurance company which gives us about £100,000 when I'm 40 or something like that. We've got an accountant who does the lot for us, and we've got different investments and things, like big companies which wouldn't go bust.

We're not ridiculous with money. The biggest thing we've got to buy this year will be houses, and a house is a good investment because the prices go up. We don't have cars except for Leslie who's bought a Ford Mustang.

You really start learning about money when you start making it. You think about it all the time. But I think where a lot of people have slipped up in the pop world is that they've thrown big parties and got this £50,000 swimming pool, and have friends over every night, and spend so many thousands of pounds on drink, and then in five years time they've got nothing. As long as you keep a steady head in this business and watch what you're doing with your money and always think about the future rather than the present then I think you'll always have money.

I keep a kitty of money. I've always done that. It's a sort of cash float really, about £200, just for odds and ends because the roadie needs money and there are other things as well.

We have a group account which is called The Bay City Rollers account, which is a sum of money in a current account just for expenses, things like paying the travel agency bill.

We don't have many personal belongings because we're always working. We will all be buying houses and everybody's bought a stereo set, which cost about £300. We buy clothes but we don't have to go out to shops any more, we get these tailors to come in. They ask you what you want, and they'll make anything up for you. We get our shoes made for us as well. One of those tartan suits we have costs between £60 and £70, but it's worth it. We usually draw what we want and we always try to keep it along the same lines. A wee bit of tartan in everything, because tartan seems to go down well, especially in America. And we'll maybe sketch something out and she'll help us. We always do our own designs.

Then we have our own hairdresser in Edinburgh called Kevin, who's been a friend of the band for a while. Every time we go home he comes to the house and cuts our hair for us. Last time when we got a haircut we were on tour and he came to the Scottish dates with us and fixed our hair.

ALAN

The biggest difference success has made to me so far is that it's really interfered with my freedom. I can never go out now, not like we used to when we lived all the time in Edinburgh. I used to like going fishing and up to the horse riding stables, but now I can't do that any more when I go home because if people see me there, they tell their friends and then I've had it.

I miss actually walking down the street and looking at shops and shopping. The last time I tried to do it, with Tam at Christmas, we got bothered all the time. We took some handout photographs with us in case we got stopped. But it became impossible.

Then another time we were in the Craig Hall studios, Edinburgh. We'd been there to make some demo records and we'd just got the bass and drums laid down. Somebody must have spotted the van or the car or something, because suddenly the place was surrounded.

There were gardens all around the studio, and across the road there was a school. Kids were swarming everywhere. At first we tried to run out and get a taxi but when the taxi driver saw all the kids he wouldn't stop. We had to go back inside and phone up the police. The whole school must have been outside. There must have been four or five hundred. The woman next door complained that all her flowers got trampled and her lawn got messed up, and they were throwing things at the windows of the studio.

I found that quite funny at the time, because at least we

were safe inside the building and we could look out of the window and see them all shouting. But sometimes it hasn't been very funny.

At a ballroom, before we started only doing concerts, I actually had my jersey ripped right off my back. My shoes were taken, and I had to run out in the gravel in my stockinged feet. My feet were all cut and bleeding and I had to try and push people back to get into the car.

That was in East Kilbride in February of 1974, and that's when I think The Rollers really started coming together. In Scotland we've always had a fan following but never anything as bad as it is now.

Mind you, we've got some really good security guys now called Artists Services. They're really clever and can get us in and out of buildings without people seeing us. It's not that we don't want to met the fans, it's just that when there's a lot of them they don't just want to say 'hello', they want to grab a piece of your shirt. It happens to everyone in the group.

All this builds up pressures on you, I suppose. Even if at first you don't notice them. I try not to let anything effect me. I'm very conscious of staying the same as I was before it all happened.

I always remember when I started off in Edinburgh and we began to get popular there a friend told me that I was going to get big-headed. I said that I didn't ever want that to happen. So I always keep a look-out for that sort of thing as far as I'm concerned. I try not to pose about the place. I just try to be myself. I hope I can just stay that way.

But sometimes it's other people who make you what you are. You get pushed around and told you must meet this or that person because they're important. 'Come here, come there. Jump in the car. Get up at eight o'clock in the morning.' And we never get back until three in the morning. I suppose it's an occupational hazard, and that's our job. Maybe in later years you can call the shots. You can say, 'Well, I don't need to go out because I'm not begging,' things like that.

I really should say that you're never too big to say 'no'. But there may be a time in the future when you don't have to get up at eight and can get up at eleven and still do the same thing. At the moment there's not enough hours in the day. In this group you've got to keep on the move and everybody's got something for you to do.

Don't get me wrong, I'm enjoying every minute of it. I mean, imagine me, just an ordinary guy from Edinburgh, and it's all happening around me and the group. But sometimes I do get to the point where I'd just like to say: 'It would be just great to get my fishing rod and my old boots and all that and just go away and do what I used to do.' I used to just get on a bus and go out of Edinburgh and have a good day. I'd take my dog with me, let the dog run about, and just sit on a river bank all day, coming back to Edinburgh at about seven or eight at night.

We used to get a few days off when we were on tour, and that was good because people didn't know when I was coming back home. I'd get out with the dog and enjoy myself. Now there's always girls outside the house. They've taken away the nameplate, they've taken the door handle, they've ripped off things here and there; they've scratched all over the walls. My dad just doesn't understand it, he doesn't taken it in, he doesn't really bother about it any more. He doesn't understand about the pop thing. He thinks it's great and he's never held me back, in fact he's always encouraged me.

He even plays a bit of piano himself. All my family are musical. Not so much my sisters, but my aunts and cousins. I've always been encouraged to be musical.

When I was younger there were always musical parties in the house. They used to have accordions, violins and the piano. The old Scottish tunes. It was really good.

I never had much confidence in myself. I've always been a bit like that. I didn't really think about taking up music until I left school. Then I used to go to dances and I wouldn't dance at all, just watch the group that was playing.

I remember when The Who came to Edinburgh. I was knocked out by the way Townshend threw his guitar all over the place, and the way he swung the microphone above himself. I was stuck right in the middle of this crowd, all the girls were screaming, and I was getting shifted along willy-nilly and all the time I was watching Townshend and trying to pick up tips.

When The Bay City Rollers first had 'Keep On Dancing' in the charts I thought: 'This is it, this is the lights and everything.' It was great at the time. But I thought you just walked on the stage and people would say, 'Oh, they're in the charts.' I was wrong. You've got to give people entertainment, and you can't walk on and play any old rubbish. You can't just play your hit and walk off. At the end, when we had 'Keep On Dancing' that's what we were doing. We never had a big act or anything and I suppose it was just inexperience. We were really big in Scotland at the time. We could fill any ballroom up there, and just play and horse around and that on stage.

When we went down to England no-one had ever heard of us, except on record. They were expecting something fantastic, which we weren't. We let them down, and I think the next record was a failure because on live gigs we never gave what we should.

Image has got a lot to do with it as well. It's done a lot for us now, but then we used to dress in suits.

Just after 'Keep On Dancing' we were getting good

money but we had to play in working men's clubs. That really killed me. I suppose it was just having a laugh together that kept us going. We always used to have a good laugh, even when we had to play way down in the West country in the holiday season. Like when we played at Torquay. We used to have this old van and we all slept in the back. We used to play football and things on the beach because you couldn't get into the hall to set up the equipment or rehearse until late in the day and we couldn't afford to stay in a hotel. We'd go down the chip shop and buy a few chips and spend the rest of the day horsing around. If somebody did have some money then we'd go to the picture house for an hour or two in the afternoon.

I've known us leave Edinburgh early on a Saturday morning at about six o'clock and travel like hell all the way to Bristol, and then right down to Torquay, sleeping on the way down. Then do the gig and sleep overnight in the van somewhere, do another gig around that area, and travel all the way back to Scotland again.

So we're finding things very different now: sleeping in hotels and having the best food. Although the past was funny at the time and we often talk among ourselves of our past experiences, I don't know if I could go back to it again.

I did have this ambition to get on all the time. It's like an apprenticeship, once you've done it and you get there, you feel that you could never go back. But I still feel as I used to and we still have a laugh. I always like to have a laugh. I've got a good sense of humour.

I realize there's a lot of opposition and it's not the getting on now, it's the keeping there, which can be just as hard. But at least we can enjoy ourselves.

It doesn't worry me at the moment – about the group having to keep there – but it may do in a year or two.

Travelling and playing live is what I really like. I always have done, even when we only appeared in Scotland.

I remember the farthest I travelled when I first started with the group. It was away in a place called Aran, a small island off the side of Glasgow in the Clyde. It was great. We were there for three days and I thought that was really travelling! Now it's quite usual for us to fly abroad.

We've had quite a few changes in the group over the years but at last we seem to have a group of guys that are settled. Some of the guys in the group in the old days used to get unsettled and they'd say after a gig: 'Let's call it a day.' I'd say that Derek and myself had packed up our jobs to make the group a full time thing and we weren't giving in, and I'd say: 'Well, I'll give it another year.' And a year would go and then I'd give it another year. A year seemed an awful long time in those days.

Just before we recorded 'Remember' we were really in debt. We all said: 'Well, this is it lads. If it doesn't go we'll just pack the whole thing in.' Tam and Derek were going to go to Australia. I didn't know what I was going to do. I didn't see me going back to being a plumber. I never wanted to do that again. I think I would have gone and worked on a farm because I've always liked animals.

Then 'Remember' did happen, and we're still here.

Now we're all thinking about the future. We've just finished this album in February, 1975, and it's been the first time that I've ultra-enjoyed myself in the studio. I've enjoyed myself playing in studios before but there's always been somebody over the top saying, 'That's wrong' and 'Do it right' and things like that. The guys we're working with now are like ourselves and they're really great. I've learned more in February of this year about being a musician than I've learned in the past three years.

We've got Phil Wainman as a producer and Colin

Fletcher as a musical arranger. He'll tell me if I'm doing right or wrong as far as my bass playing in relationship to the other instruments is concerned, and he's really great with harmonies. He won't let you off anything either. He'll say, 'That's a bit flat', but it's just the way we worked together.

I had a great laugh in the studios, speaking through the talkback to the producers box and things like that. We made the album and single at Chipping Norton in Oxfordshire. There's a house right next to the studio, where you stay, with a dart board upstairs. If you've done your part and you get fed-up hanging around you can go and play darts or watch the telly or whatever you want to do. But in normal studios up in London you go in and you can never come out again till night.

I think in the next two years we'll be playing the same danceable music because we enjoy playing it. I hope to write songs like Eric and Woody do now.

Actually we all help each other, but I'd like to write a song on my own. I've got a few songs written, but they're not really good. I hope the group stays together so that even if someone does something on his own they'll still be with the group.

I've not really thought about what I want to do yet. But I don't think it will be musical. Maybe I'd like to do something with horses. I love horses very much and I enjoy riding. Maybe I'll be involved with a farm or something like that.

I've been interested in horses ever since I was at school in Edinburgh. There were gypsies who used to stay outside the city. They had ponies and horses for the wealthier people to go for a trek across the hills on a Sunday. Well, I used to clean up the stables and do lots of other jobs and then when the people had returned I'd take the horses back to the stables and take their saddles off and ride them bareback up to the field. I used to get paid for my work as well, which was good. That's how I learned to ride.

Three or four of my mates at school used to do the same thing. In Edinburgh there are horses that pull the milk carts around, and I used to work cleaning them. I would take the horses down from the stables to the blacksmith and back, and ride them a lot. That was good fun as well. It's a great feeling being on a horse. I can't really explain it, but you feel very free and alone together.

I still try to see those same mates but it's a lot harder now, of course. I try to keep in touch with them by writing although I'm not very good at sending letters. I get letters from them too.

There were girlfriends in those days as well, but I seem to have lost contact with them. I sometimes look back and think it must be funny for them to see me on television. They'll probably be saying: 'Look at that idiot. I used to go out with that guy.'

The trouble is that, once again, when we're back in Scotland we just don't get the chance to pop out and look somebody up. And when we are home there's so much to be done, like all the washing, and sorting out the clothes for the next journey, and all those ordinary sort of things that you don't get much time to do.

I'm looking for a place now outside Edinburgh, so that'll improve things. Some of my mates will be able to come there and help me fix it all up.

The only chance I get to meet girls these days is just like when we met Princess Anne at the Carl Alan Awards. You just say, 'How do you do', and that's it, 'Goodnight', and you're away.

Then at concerts, we get a lot of mail backstage which we go through before we go on. There's usually quite a lot of presents, and we've got to get things ready. There are always interviewers to see.

By that time we're due on stage, so there's no chance of meeting anyone. We go on stage, then we come off, then out the back door, away back to the hotel, go to sleep or have a drink or something, and then away again the next morning to the next place.

Maybe in about another year or so we'll have a bit more time to ourselves and we can start meeting people again.

It's an odd world we live in. You can't really explain it to anyone outside. I'd like to see what other people think, looking in at the group now. It's funny when girls come up to you and they start crying and they talk to you and you feel like saying: 'I'm just the same as you really,' but they never see it that way. Personally I always feel: 'Who the hell am I? I'm just an ordinary guy from Edinburgh that's maybe made it on television.'

It's very strange.

WOODY

I went to school until I was sixteen and then left and became an electrician. I always secretly wanted to be a pop
star, but I didn't tell anyone.

I'd been in groups since I was about fourteen, and I
kept up playing after I left school. One of the groups I
played for was Kip, which was managed by Tam Paton.

During that first year when I worked as an electrician
by day and in the group by night, life was very tiring.

Well, you can imagine having to get up early in the
morning to go to work after playing with the group all
night, and so some days I didn't turn up until nearer
lunchtime. I used to get into trouble for that.

I was the last one to join The Rollers, in January of
1974. It was a bit strange, because I didn't know any of
them except Eric. I was shy, very shy at first, but I've got
a lot less shy as the months have gone by. I think the
success of the group has brought me out of myself a bit.
They're very nice guys to be with, and everyone in The
Rollers helps everyone else. I'd known Tam for some time,
and he looks after us very well.

Nowadays, of course, we can't get out very much. I
spend most of my time practising and writing songs. If
there's a swimming pool in the hotel where we're staying
you won't keep me out of it for very long, because that's
one of my greatest relaxations. I love swimming.

I used to be in a swimming club before I joined The
Rollers. I swam for my school, so you can see I'm quite

serious about it. I think everyone should learn how to swim, because if you live in a city, like we did in Edinburgh, it's a simple way of getting exercise. Also if you ever go abroad or down to the seaside you're quite safe.

At school my two interests were swimming and music. I started to learn music in my first year at secondary school. The first instrument I ever played was the recorder. I'd always wanted to play the trumpet, but I started out on the recorder, which is a good instrument to begin with.

Then I had a go on the trumpet but I got sick of that so I moved on to the cornet. I got sick of that as well.

A few other guys at my school wanted to start a group, so I got a few books on guitar playing out of the library and bought myself a second hand guitar for £2.

It didn't have any strings.

I put some new strings on it and started to teach myself.

Somebody or other in my family's past had been on the stage, but no-one else had been musical or anything like that.

I got so keen on learning the guitar that I had private lessons at home in my time off from school. I was lucky because one of our neighbours was musical and he just came round and gave me lessons. It was hard to pick it all up at first. There was a piano in the house too, because my brother was studying the piano, and that made things easier.

I started out playing things like 'Frere Jacques', very simple songs. I played that for about two years.

At one time I could have joined the school orchestra, but I didn't like all that orchestral stuff. I preferred jazzy sounding trumpets. Anyway, I never mastered the trumpet. I knew I always wanted to play pop music.

And now I'm with The Rollers, that's all I want to be doing. People ask about the future. Well, my mind is in the present. But when I look at the future I hope the group's success will last for eight or nine years. After that I'd like to stay in the music business either writing songs or managing groups.

That's what I'd like to do. I've just got to hope.

People think it's an embarrassment being a teeny pop group, but where would we be without our fans? I think it's great being a teeny pop group and seeing all those girls out there, and sometimes meeting them.

There was a competition in a magazine for girls to meet us backstage and have their picture taken with us. They got the picture in the local press. These girls interviewed us as part of the prize.

So we do sometimes meet fans, and they meet us. Mind you, it's not always as simple as that. I've seen girls get overcome when we come face to face, because the only time they've seen us before was on the telly or on stage, and they can't bear the actual meeting. Then other girls are perfectly natural. I suppose it just depends on what sort of girl she is.

The questions they ask us are always the same. How old are we? How many pairs of baggies have I got? What football team do I support?

The answer to that last question is that I used to support Hibernian, but I don't get time to go and watch football matches any more. I'm still a Hibs supporter, all the same.

As for my clothes, which I think most of the fans want to know about, I keep more or less the same fashion going all the time at present. I just get different designs on the same theme. We have boots with a white stripe, or there might be a different coloured strip. For example, I had the idea to have the letter W on my boots, and I have them hand made, which costs about £34 a pair. Then I have sort of sports shoes which cost £12 a pair.

I've always been interested in clothes. I spend quite a lot of thought on them now. I think clothes are important. At school I used to wear jeans turned up, and then when I joined The Rollers they were all wearing striped trousers. I suppose clothes are the thing I spend most money on at the moment – not that I spend much money. I've bought myself a stereo and quite a few records because I couldn't afford to have many records before, and I really like listening to music at home.

But the trouble is that the stereo is too big to carry around with me, so the only time I can hear it is when I'm at home. I like Paul McCartney and Status Quo. I've always collected records, although as I've said, I couldn't afford many in the past. But in my collection I've got some old 78s which are among my most valuable possessions.

As we can't really go out nowadays I don't have much opportunity of spending money. I suppose I could buy a car, or anything I like, but there's not much point buying something unless you're going to be able to use it. The main things I'm going to get are a house and a small car. Once you've got a house you can buy this and that for it, but at the moment it's all a bit pointless.

The house will be in Scotland. I think it'll be in a nice district of Edinburgh because I like Edinburgh very much as a place to live. It's a very beautiful city. I don't think I'd like to live in London, though. Up in Edinburgh you can get fresh air but I've never found that with London, I always feel a bit filthy there. It's not a very clean place.

'resenting the Bay City Rollers ... Britain's best loved pop group

Stuart John Wood ... "Woody" to his thousands of fans

Leslie McKeown … "I get a buzz from making people happy"

Eric Faulkner…"my parents wanted me to do classical music."

Derek Longmuir..."once we had 200 girls outside our house."

Alan Longmuir ... a lot of weight on his mind at a health farm

Three of the boys getting fit. Can you recognize them?

The five shining knights at Roscoe's Round Table.

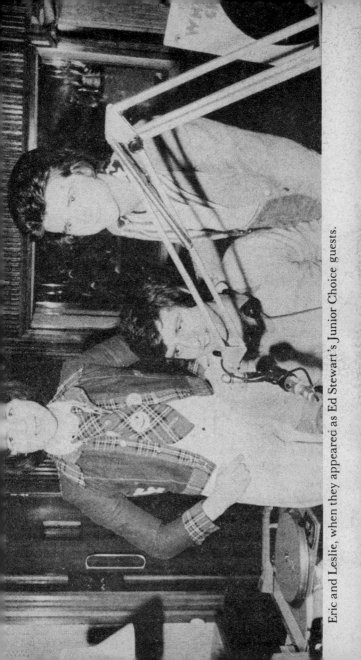

Eric and Leslie, when they appeared as Ed Stewart's Junior Choice guests.

How times change! This is Eric a few years ago ...

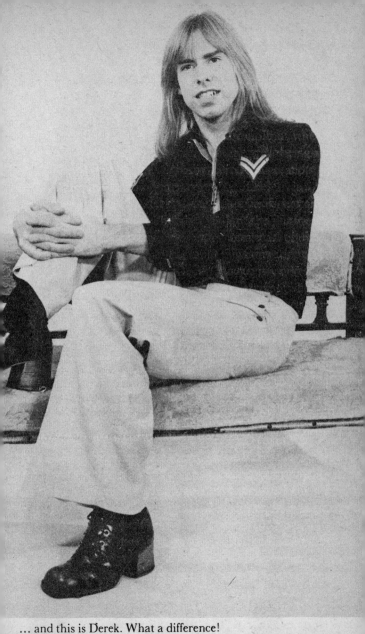

... and this is Derek. What a difference!

Tam Paton (left) with TV personality Michael Wale who wrote the bo

Woody receives a silver disc on Michael's show.

Shots from the past. Derek and Alan with the original Rollers

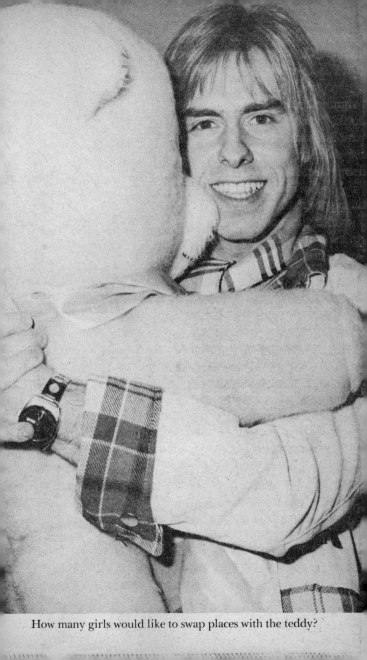

How many girls would like to swap places with the teddy?

The cuddly Rollers – with some cuddly toys. Steady on, girls!

ERIC

I suppose my parents would have liked me to be a classical musician.

When I was at school I used to play the violin in the school orchestra. I even managed to get a place in the Edinburgh Schools Orchestra.

It was pretty competitive at the time, because there are a lot of schools in Edinburgh. Only me and a girl were chosen to represent my school. At about the age of 13 I remember playing for the Edinburgh Schools Orchestra in front of the Queen Mother, and lining up afterwards to meet her, and her saying she'd enjoyed it and everything. That gave me a real buzz.

By then I'd started to learn the guitar as well. But I broke my left wrist trying to swing over a river on a rope – I fell off – and that stopped me playing for about two months.

We formed our own group at school, called Witness. We started off just doing school dances, and after six months we actually managed to get a van together. We got some gigs up as far as Dundee for about £15 a night, which wasn't bad as we were all thirteen and fourteen at the time.

That's how I came to give up the orchestra. All the late nights with the group just didn't leave the time to practise.

As soon as I'd sat my O-levels I left school. I got six of them, by the way: music, maths, biology, chemistry, English and English literature. My parents were in two minds at the time: they were disappointed that I'd decided to leave school, because they obviously wanted me to go to university or something.

On the other hand they could see I was enjoying myself in the group and we were beginning to earn money.

They helped me a lot, as a matter of fact. They spent all their money on amplifiers, and there was a time when my mother actually paid out £70 insurance on a van when I was in a group called Sugar.

In fact, my parents were always doing things like that, helping out with hire purchase agreements. They used to open letters at home which started off: 'Your payment on such and such is due now.' But it all added up to fun in those days.

Then we met Tam. We changed the name of Sugar to Kip, and for a year I worked on his lorry, delivering to shops around Edinburgh.

I don't regret never having been to university, and I still keep up the violin. I played it on one track on our first album, and it'll be used on our second. I don't think I could actually play any classical stuff on it any more. The sort of things we played when I was in the orchestra were pretty basic, but it's been useful having that background because I can read music. I'm always getting books out of the library about arranging for orchestras. That'll help me in the future. Arranging fascinates me. It's very involved.

My parents are now pleased about the choice I've made, and I'm able to buy them a house. In fact, I think everybody in the group is going to help their parents because they were all very good to us when we were struggling.

And we've had some struggles, believe you me. For example there was a time in August, 1973, when I thought it was all going to end as far as The Rollers were concerned. I'd left home because my parents had gone to live in Grangemouth. I was sixteen, and I stayed with my aunt for four months then got myself some digs.

I stayed in thousands of places – bedsits, a caravan, and all sorts of dumps. I'd been on the road with The Rollers for about a year, and everybody was beginning to think that we'd never make it. And I was in a real dump right then. So there I was. I'd left school and I'd left home and I was just one of the thousands as far as being in a group was concerned.

We'd actually come to the point where we'd rather pack it all in. Alan wanted to go back to his job and Derek wanted to be a joiner again. We didn't want to practise.

Somehow we came through it all, but it was very close to the end.

I think it is being on the road that wears you down. You do get very tired. It's not so bad now, because we can stay in good places and travel comfortably, but in those days it was there and back overnight in the van.

The process destroys any private life you might have. I mean, you can't have a relationship with one woman because you're never in the same place two days running. We're hardly ever home in Edinburgh any more. You've got to accept that, and you can hardly expect a girl to wait for you all that time.

We're 100 per cent involved in the group. At the moment we're working on the album, and when you're in the studio that's all you do besides eat and sleep. After that we'll be getting ideas for our new stage act – we've got ideas about the films we want projecting around us – and all this time we'll be on the move and away from home.

Then there will be America. And then we're on tour again, and afterwards it's time for another album. So you can see what I mean : where's the time to have a relationship with a girl that really is lasting? I don't think any girl could put up with all this.

And that's how it's going to be for the next three years. Obviously I'd love to have a relationship with a girl, and I'm sure all the group would, but you can't have your cake and eat it.

Then there's the pressures that success has brought us. I feel at the moment that everyone is watching us. Watching from the sidelines to see what our next album is like, especially because we've just changed writers and producers.

There's always people around the music business who would like you to fall flat on your face. It's good press and all that, something to talk about. I think we're firmly established as an act now, because of the way we look, et cetera, but I don't think we've done anything remarkable musically. We'd be the first to admit that.

Things will change very much in the future. One of the pressures will be on us as writers, because people want to see if we can write songs. That's good for us, because it makes us try harder.

If something is wrong we're the first to admit it. A critic wrote something once about our sound equipment. We bumped it up to 6,000 watts by the next concert.

The album provides the pressures on us at the moment. Live concerts aren't any worry because our audience is there and we all enjoy it.

Another pressure is just hanging about. We can't go out because we'd be mobbed, so we have to stay cooped up in this hotel at the moment. That can get a bit boring. Still, we're all here together which means a lot. We get on very well together. We talk quite a bit about the past and have a good laugh.

For example, when I first joined The Rollers I wouldn't be earning more than £7 a week. There were times I wouldn't have any money for meals, so I'd go up to Alan and Derek's.

Things were very rough on stage for us in those days, so you'd need a good meal inside you.

There was a time I was nearly killed.

I'd be about fifteen at the time. We were playing in this place in Edinburgh. Half way through our set something went inside my guitar. There was a big flash and sparks flew about everywhere. There was terrible-smelling smoke, and kids screamed, and I looked down at my hands and I couldn't take them off the strings.

Both my hands were stuck to my guitar and they just started shaking. I'm not exaggerating, but if it were not for someone pulling me away I would have been killed. Someone pulled the plug out from the mains and everything stopped.

I just stood there shaking at the thought of what had happened. Rock musicians have been killed on stage before.

There was another night when the whole group was attacked.

We were playing just outside Edinburgh. A gang in the hall suddenly got up on stage and started smashing all the gear. The Hammond organ was hurled off the stage. I remember smashing my guitar over a guy's head. Everyone was fighting.

The police came in, and the bouncers were fighting off this gang too. Girls were hitting them with handbags, it was just chaos. When it was over, all we had left was our guitars.

One of the roadies had to go to hospital to have stitches

put in his head where he'd been hit with a mike stand. It was just like the Wild West films.

Quite a lot of that happened in the early days of The Rollers because we had to appear in some really rough places. Still, it toughened us up for the future. This was in the days when The Rollers was just a group for girls, and their guys used to get very jealous. They'd always try to attack us just before we were due to leave the stage.

Everyone got a bashing then. We've all had blows on the head and in the face. There was one Christmas Eve, I remember, when a guy just came up on stage and sat down on Derek's drums. Derek was quite reasonable, and politely asked him to get off so he could continue to play.

Quite suddenly there were hundreds of guys swarming up on to the stage and bashing everything in sight, which included us! We had to fight our way out the back and into the van.

Not for the first time, Tam got injured that night. As a matter of fact I've seen him on the floor with fellows belting him before now. He's pretty tough, our manager, and he can usually get out of any scrape. But he used to be in a real dodgy situation because he had to be in front of the stage. It was much easier for us up on the stage. People used to leap on his back and everything. He's had stitches in cuts before now, defending us.

One night I broke my Gibson 335 guitar on some guy's head. The neck broke off, and it was a £300 guitar. Amplifiers and mikes were always getting smashed, and we didn't have much money to replace them, so we used to fight hard as much to save our equipment as anything else.

It's like that in certain areas of Scotland. If you went to Aberdeen, for example, there would be no trouble, but in Shotts, Motherwell, East Kilbride, Glasgow and those places they start to get a bit rough.

Gangs were very much in the news in Scotland in those days. It's quieter now. I'd say though, in an odd way, it was the best thing that ever happened for us. If we'd had it easy it wouldn't be the same at all. If we'd had someone come along and say he had £50,000 to invest in the band, we wouldn't have had the tough working pressure behind us to succeed.

Even when I was in little groups before I joined The Rollers there was always this terrific rivalry between us all. We used to get up to all sorts of tricks. Like if we arrived when another group was on stage we'd switch off the mains, and things like that. But it was all a game really. The groups were fighting each other and it made the groups better.

Things are very different for us now that we're well known. Mind you, there is this Rollermania thing. If you can call it that. I'd say it will last for three or four more years.

After that it's really got to be the music. It's going to be that because in a few years' time someone younger than us will be doing the same thing we are now, and it's really up to us. If we can write good enough songs and play well enough, then we'll last. If we can't . . .

It's really up to us. The ball is at our feet. If we don't make the grade, it's only our fault. But I think as it is at the moment it will last a good few years. We're obviously going to advance as the years go on.

I write songs, Leslie is starting to write songs, and so is Woody. It's a thing we're getting interested in.

I'd like always to be involved in music and everything around it. I'd like to get into record production. Maybe in about five years' time I'll be able to go into a recording studio with some other act and work with them and produce them.

We're still in the middle of all this Rollermania, as I call it, so we don't think of the future that much. I mean, you have to hear our fans to believe what goes on. You're standing there waiting to go on stage there's so much noise in the audience! There's the screams, and the banner-waving, and the scarves, and everything.

You've got to have had that happen to you to know what it's like. It makes you feel really good. You get a sort of funny feeling inside of you. It makes my hair stand on end.

On the last tour we used a tape to start the act. The tape lasted just three minutes, and we found that waiting terrible. So I can imagine what it was like for the audience.

So we're just sort of standing there and it builds up on us and when we walk on, the noise just erupts. It's a feeling you just can't describe. It makes everything worth it. When it happens you forget everything that might ever have gone wrong.

Then all the fans are leaping up and screaming. I suppose they do this because they read all about us in the magazines, and they see photographs, then suddenly here we are in person.

Everybody must have an idol. Everybody seems to accept that we're the new Beatles and that we're doing the exact same thing. We've done the same venues as The Beatles, and the same concert tours. There's people saying: 'Oh, I've never seen this reaction since The Beatles,' and things like that.

We very much admire what The Beatles did. I can really only remember the Beatles since their albums 'Revolver' and 'Sergeant Pepper'. Everyone has to have idols. It's like when guys go to a football match and all scream and yell and shout. They're having a good time really, which is a good thing.

It's certainly great standing on stage when somebody comes up and grabs you and it's a good laugh. Everybody thinks it's really dangerous, and I suppose it is, but we enjoy it.

DOWN AND OUT – AGAIN

I felt the boys needed to get away from it all.

They'd taken this last failure pretty personally and I couldn't keep their spirits going for ever in the hope we'd get a hit. Since we'd had a hit with 'Keep on Dancing' our records were expected to make an impact almost immediately or that was the end of them. And as far as 'Manana' was concerned, it was the end of that. So no matter, we decided to take a holiday.

As with anything concerned with The Rollers it was to be no ordinary holiday. Not for us the glossy brochures and packaged holiday where a jet takes you to some golden beaches in the sun. All meals included. No, for us we had to work it all out on the slender budget available. First we looked at our assets. Well, we can all cook a bit, and we did have a van, so we decided to load up the van with food, and drive to Spain. Simple when you read it on the printed page, isn't it? Simple? You must be joking.

First of all, we drove our van down to the local Cash and Carry and bought all the food. This involved a few arguments in itself because no one could quite agree on what food we should take. I pleaded that we should keep it all simple. It had to be the sort of thing that could be heated and slapped on plates.

As I tell you this, I can just hear the grunts and groans from our roadie Jake, who is a qualified chef and insists on using all fresh vegetables when he's doing the cooking. Jake acted as chef when we made our second album in

January this year at Chipping Norton studios up in Oxfordshire. It's a great studio because we actually slept in a house within the studio and we had our own cooking facilities. When Jake was away, I was in charge of the kitchen – and he'd come back to find all these tins which would drive him mad. He's a really great cook.

His speciality is home-made soup. Mmmm, it makes my mouth water just to think about it. The favourite with the group while we were making the album was leek soup. Jake had gone out first thing and bought all these fresh leeks. But back to the more mundane days of The Rollers shopping for the great Spanish invasion . . .

We bought these huge cans of Irish stew and as all The Rollers like chips, my dad supplied us with several bags of potatoes. We got a sack of rice and these huge cans of soup, plus tins of fruit, and we piled it all in the van. What we couldn't get inside we put on the roof. I think we spent about £30 on food altogether, which wasn't bad at all considering there were six of us.

We planned for fourteen days' holiday altogether and eight of those days would be spent on the road going and coming back.

The only Roller who is fussy with food is Leslie. He is very fussy. He'll look at his food and think: 'I don't want this, I don't want that.' He'll play about with it on a fork and when I see him doing that I know he doesn't like the food. He's got a conscience, and feels that if he has ordered it, he has got to eat it. If he sees something on the menu with a strange name, he'll order it without knowing what it is. When it turns up he'll say quite simply: 'Oh, I don't like that.' Thank goodness he wasn't with us on the Spanish trip!

The rest of The Rollers weren't bothered. We had been

on the road so long and had got used to eating in some pretty terrible places.

When we went into transport cafes we'd all order the same because we always ran this kitty. We each got £6 a week and out of that we'd have to pay our digs, which usually meant £5 a week to our mums, so that left a pound. I smoked, and I had to buy my cigarettes out of that. Nobby and John Devine smoked as well, but the others didn't. Derek ran the kitty and when we went into one of these cafes he would pay. We used to line up one behind the other and go down the self-service with our trays and we'd all tell each other: 'Everybody try to get the same.' If one person got a plate of soup then everyone would get soup. This was to make it easy for Derek at the end. Instead of having a complicated order to settle up he would just look down at his tray and then multiply it by the number of people with us that night.

That's the great thing about The Rollers – they really are a team. They do everything together and it makes things much easier. Even today, in posh hotels, it's the same – and I know it stems back to those days queueing up in transport cafes.

So one sunny morning our van drove out of Edinburgh again on its longest journey. It was weighed down by food, not by equipment for a change, and we all just sighed a big sigh of relief. We needed a break from it all, and at last here we were away from all the pressures of having to struggle. Now we could just enjoy ourselves in the Spanish sunshine.

A ferry took us over to France and very soon we pulled up beside a main road, got out our stove and had our first meal on foreign soil. Everyone was joking and laughing, because we weren't too clever at setting up our makeshift kitchen. But because the weather was so wonderful it didn't matter. It's amazing what sunshine can do for people. We were all pale and tired from our experiences of the past two years, but now we just stretched out contentedly at the side of the road, and put our worries out of our minds.

I must confess I did not share in the cooking. I'd realized early in life that I was really hopeless at it. The extent of my cookery talent was boiling a couple of eggs. And even then I think I'd get the timing wrong. Alan was the best cook, so he was in charge of getting all the gas cookers and things together. We'd help, and then he'd take over.

Derek and Eric mucked about with the cooking too. Mind you, sometimes I ate one of their meals without knowing what it was. So I don't think there were any budding chefs among the group really. It ended up one night with us eating cold rice because we'd run out of gas. That almost made me sick, but the boys assured me it was good for us. Another time, they put the chips in the pan before the oil was hot enough so we had these terrible soggy chips. And the eggs! We bought eggs from farmhouses along the way and the boys never seemed to get them right.

We'd stop anywhere and cook up on the spot. Once we actually stopped in a French town and ate on the side of the pavement. No one seemed to mind. In fact, it proved quite an attraction for the locals.

It was all on the cheap, although I know all the lads had been slipped a tenner by their parents before they set off. So at least they could buy one or two little extras along the way.

It wasn't long before our usual travel trouble struck again. Because the weather was so warm and our van was used to the cold British winters, the engine began to boil up more and more. We'd have to stop several times a day while it cooled down and steam poured out of the engine. It looked really bad at times and we began to wonder if we'd ever reach Spain. But the old van always got going again. Now our speed was cut down to a mere twenty-five miles an hour as we got nearer and nearer the French-Spanish border. Alongside the road the heat shimmered on the brown grass and vehicles passed us every few seconds in clouds of dust as they sped on their way. Our poor old van limped on and on.

We felt we would have to crawl our way over the Pyrenees, the mountain range that divides the South of France and Spain. There was this terrible heat and steam coming almost continually from underneath the bonnet. The engine sound had been reduced to something like the chugging of a very loud motor boat and the steam also made a hissing sound. Our excitement was beginning to wane a bit under this stress. It was like one of the many war films we'd seen when a British bomber is limping back to base on one engine. Will it get back in time or crash? We felt exactly the same suspense – only this was for real, and our first holiday was beginning to vanish before our eyes. Derek got quieter than ever. Alan's natural sense of humour wasn't bubbling as usual. And Eric just looked out at the sun and sighed.

Yet there was a funny side to it all, and that was how we must have appeared to the local people. Imagine it: a spluttering, steaming old van, crammed with people, with food piled high on the roof. We had no shirts on and were sitting there as if we were on the Queen Mary or something. Just like big wealthy tourists. The sun was so strong that some of the lads got badly sunburned. Alan and Eric were bad, but Derek's burns were really drastic. One of the luxuries we couldn't really afford was suntan lotion, so we all looked pretty pink. Which must have made us all look even funnier.

Every now and again we had to stop as we slowly climbed up the mountain road and everyone would pour out of the van and run to get some shade from the pine trees. In some ways that part of the journey was frightening, too, because the road up the Pyrenees curls round and round like a spiral staircase and just as you're approaching yet another bend a car comes thundering down on the other side of the road. They're really mad drivers out there. And if anything went wrong there's a sheer drop thousands of feet below.

But that sort of road does have one great advantage, especially when you're in an old van. As soon as we reached the top, we gave the van yet another perspiring rest, then switched off the engine and coasted all the way down into Spain. You should never do this, of course. It is extremely dangerous because the vehicle can easily get out of control, but I'm afraid as far as The Rollers and myself were concerned it was either that or kiss our holiday goodbye. The van would never have been able to make it without that long cooling descent spiralling down the mountains.

When we arrived at the border the Customs men could hardly believe their eyes. In fact, they were very friendly. They burst out laughing and, with a solemn salute, welcomed us to Spain. We felt like lords, and even the van seemed to take new heart as it chugged faithfully along the final miles to the spot on the coast where we planned to stop.

I'll never forget the moment we reached the road alongside the Mediterranean. The sea was as blue as it is on every holiday postcard. So was the sky. It was like heaven. The back-doors of the van suddenly burst open. All the boys jumped out and raced across the golden sand on the beach and straight into the water, in their jeans, splashing each other, falling over in the waves, rolling and swimming around. I had never seen the group so happy.

There were all these people in deckchairs under large umbrellas. They must have been quite disgusted at the time because so keen were the boys to get into the water that they ran in a straight line from the van, right through them. It must have given everyone quite a shock. I just stayed in the van at first watching them. I was secretly praying that the van would finally get us back to Scotland when our holiday was over.

We hired a small flat right there and then at the first place we had stopped for five days, and we had a great time. The boys went on the beach all day every day and told everybody that they were The Bay City Rollers who had been in the charts with 'Keep On Dancing'. And everyone replies: 'Who? What's that name again? The Straws?' You see, they couldn't understand the boy's Scots accents. And then at night we'd all go into the local discotheques and wait for one of our records to come up on the jukebox. But they never did.

We got our flat really cheap because the landlord liked the group. He thought they were a very funny bunch of people jumping about all over the place with only their jeans on, and he charged us only about £7 for our whole stay. Which was almost unbelievable.

Gradually, Derek, Alan and Eric turned a great golden brown and began to look very different sorts of people. Of course none of us had any money at all, so the boys were always trying to get rides on horses on the beach for nothing. Alan would lead the way and plead: 'How's about a trip for nothing? No money.' He managed it, too. We all had our own horses two or three times and we had a great laugh acting being cowboys and all that sort of thing.

All too soon the moment we had been dreading arrived: the time to return to Scotland. We were having such a wonderful time we didn't want the holiday to end. But we had to go, so we packed everything into the van and drove off.

As the van chugged off towards France, it was obvious that things were even worse than when we battled our way over the Pyrenees. And after we'd crossed the border, it conked out for the last time. All efforts to start it again failed, and so we wheeled it into the side of the road, unpacked as much food as we could carry and left it there.

I often wonder what happened to that poor old van. For all I know it's still there beside that French road. I only hope whoever found it finally was kind to it, and it ended up as some use to someone. It had certainly given us great service, and it was quite sad to leave it there.

As for us, we decided to split up into pairs and start hitching back to the Channel boat many hundreds of miles away. We did this because we thought that six long-haired people in a group would never get a lift. And it was really strange because soon we were passing each other in all sorts of vehicles. Derek and I got a lift quickly in a lorry, but were soon passed by Alan and Eric, sitting snugly in the back of a smart car. They gave us a smug smile and a wave.

Surprisingly, we got back to the Channel port in a day and a half – a lot quicker than we would have done in the van. Alan and Eric arrived first and we were all a bit dirty and dishevelled. It hadn't all been a smooth return. I remember one night Derek and myself were in this French town in the South. We were really hungry and we had hardly any money as usual. Suddenly we came upon these wonderful chickens rotating on a spit by the pavement. For one moment we were tempted to take one, but then we both said out loud at the same time: 'No.' We have never believed in stealing – even in our poorest days. So we stayed hungry.

It was quite uncanny really how we all arrived at the port within a matter of hours of each other. We hadn't planned it that way. But there you are – The Rollers always seem to stick together.

Of course, we didn't have enough money on the boat to book those lovely armchairs where you can just go to sleep, which is what we felt like doing after nearly two days of continuous hitch-hiking. So we just huddled down on the deck. Fortunately, it was a warm night. When we arrived back in Britain we didn't even have the money for the train ticket to London, so we split into twos and started hitching again. I think experiences like these underline what a struggle The Rollers had to succeed. I don't think anyone would have believed that a group that had been on Top of the Pops several times and appeared all over Britain were right now thumbing their way to London. But that was the truth.

In fact, we hitched lifts around London and on towards Newcastle. When we arrived there we were brown, filthy and dirty, and we'd gone through nearly all the food we'd salvaged from the van. When we finally arrived in Edinburgh my mother hardly recognized these brown dirty little fellows. That night was the best and longest night's sleep I think any of us have ever had. Nowadays, I don't normally get to bed before three or even four in the morning; I just can't go to sleep if I go any earlier. Anyway, I find the calm quiet stillness of the early hours a very good time to catch up on my work. Phones don't usually ring then. But that night I was in bed well before midnight and slept right through till quite late the next day. It had been a great holiday, but we were back now, refreshed, and ready to take on the pop world again in our fight to become the stars.

'SATURDAY NIGHT'

For our next record Bell had decided that Bill Martin and Phil Coulter, who had written the Eurovision winning song, 'Puppet On A String', and also many other hits throughout the world, would take over production.

By then, Eric had started writing with Nobby, and I thought some of their songs were pretty good. But Bill Martin came up with a number called 'Saturday Night', which he felt would be a smash hit. The group wanted to have one of their own songs on the 'B' side – not only to earn themselves a bit more money but because they wanted to write more of their own material – but Bill refused. He implied that they should be grateful for small mercies; he was giving us a song and that was that. As we'd had two failures since 'Keep On Dancing', we couldn't really argue.

When we arrived at the studios a backing track had already been laid down and the boys were told to sing over it. We felt this was a bit depressing. We'd had only one hit and this was our fourth record, and I felt The Rollers were being pushed to the side. But at the time I didn't feel I could say anything because I was really starting to worry about the whole future of The Rollers. Although we'd had a holiday and had a great time I was beginning to think it was all coming to an end. I was just grateful we were getting another try. I honestly believed that if 'Saturday Night' didn't happen we'd be finished. So I spoke to the group one by one to impress on them the importance of this recording session.

I said to Nobby: 'Try not to worry. Just let's go ahead and do it and calm things down, and let's persevere and get it done.' It was the backing track that had upset him in particular. Plus the fact that he had written these songs with Eric and none of them were being used.

The backing track had been put down because the record people thought it would save money. But it was a very difficult moment, and I know the group didn't want to work like that. I must admit I got very angry and had kicked up a fuss.

It was one of the few arguments I've had with the group, but I had to impress on them that they were in danger of becoming one-hit wonders. You see, if Bill had decided to finish with them it would have been very difficult to get another recording contract.

I had a lot of aggro with Nobby at the time and it all became very depressing. By this time I was between £2,000 and £3,000 in debt, despite the fact that we were working hard and playing nearly every night.

Although we always tried to make it back to Edinburgh at night, or sleep in the van, this wasn't always possible or desirable – and it was at this time that we started something that we even continue today. That is, we always book double rooms, and two of us sleep in each room. In the case of Woody, it is a necessity because he is still very frightened of the dark, but it's good for the others too because the boys keep themselves company and nobody gets depressed or lonely. The only couple who don't share are Derek and Alan because they're brothers. They always share with either Leslie or Eric or myself or Woody. Well, you know how it is with brothers, even if they are the best of friends most of the time.

Mind you, in the beginning we had a few frights as far as hotels are concerned. I always remember the time in

London when we stayed at this place which wasn't exactly
The Dorchester. This big Irish chap took us to our rooms.
He said, 'Two in here. And two in here.' We each paired
off, then he said: 'And we'll have three in this room. Yes,
I think this room will take three.' I walked in with Eric
just to see if it would be all right for him and there were
fourteen beds in the room. Fourteen beds! I couldn't believe it. It was like a barrack room, and you could have
rolled from bed to bed and there were men lying there.
Needless to say we spent the night outside in the van – we
couldn't face a room with fourteen in it. The trouble was
that the guy said we'd booked in and took our money.

That was at the time we were making 'Saturday Night'.
We slept in the van and went back inside the place to get a
wash in the morning. Then we went in and recorded all
day and returned to the van at night to sleep. When we
had finished the record we retreated to Scotland. Things
were becoming really quite drastic, and once again we
found we were known in Scotland but hardly known at all
in England. Then we got an offer to go to Belfast, which
seemed a bit of a sick joke at the time. I suppose, in truth,
nobody else would go there because of all the bombing and
shooting but we decided that we'd have to go because the
money we'd been offered just could not be refused. I
reasoned that once we got over there we'd have our own
van and our expenses would be quite low.

We had brought a new Mercedes van by then because
we just could not risk breaking down. A lot of people
would say that it was bad management to buy a new van
when we were so much in debt, but it proved to be a long-
term investment. We had to have a van to tour, so we
thought we might as well get a good one.

We all piled into this nice new van and went across the
sea to Ireland. We were worried about it because the

troubles there were at their peak. We thought it would be quite dangerous, and we were really pretty frightened, but we didn't let on to anyone.

When we landed in Dublin we were a bit tired because we had had to sleep in deckchairs on the boat. It had been a night journey and we had got pretty cold. I can assure you the middle of the Irish Channel in the middle of the night can be a pretty cold place. I could almost hear Eric's teeth chattering.

But our first audience in Dublin more than made it up to us. We played a place called The Revolution Club and everyone was so nice it was amazing. Then we motored over to the West coast and played in Galway, a very beautiful city, built on a bay, and nobody had a clue who The Bay City Rollers were.

We advertised ourselves as 'Scotland's Top Group', adding 'Hit Makers of Keep On Dancing'. But by this time even those who came along to see the group couldn't remember our one and only hit.

After Galway and one or two other places we went North. We were getting very good money to do this and we needed it. We were booked to play every night, which was quite fantastic because it meant us earning about £1,000.

We played in Bangor, just outside Belfast and as we crossed the border at Newry I thought: 'God Almighty. What's this?' There was this big metal barrier with wee slots in it. A big soldier came up and said: 'Where have you come from? Have you got a driving licence? Have you got your passport?' I said: 'We're The Bay City Rollers.' His face was expressionless. 'Yeah, fine. What are you, a group or something?' He thought we were a basketball team. That was the height of our fame. Imagine people saying: 'Are you a basketball team?'

Anyway it was frightening right from the moment we crossed the border, because this soldier also carried a machine gun, and suddenly you realized that the troubles were very real indeed.

One night when we were returning from a gig I had told our driver – a wee Irish guy – to put his foot down – when suddenly, on the road from Antrim to Belfast, this big van drew up alongside. It was the police. I told the driver I would do the talking as it might go down better if they realized I was a visitor. But the driver insisted he dealt with it. We all had to get out onto the road and a policeman kept a machine gun trained on us all the time, he asked us questions.

The boys couldn't believe it. As soon as they were told they could go, they said: 'Let's get out of here quick.'

Fortunately that was the only time we were really bothered by anyone because they realized we weren't political. We got the wildest receptions at all our concerts because very few groups would dare to play in Northern Ireland. If ever we were asked about the group's religion, I'd say that half were Protestant and half were Catholic. In fact that visit was so good for us that we went back several times afterwards. To let you into a secret, we didn't realize that every other group refused to play in Northern Ireland, so we just kept going back as if they were normal gigs. And each time we've returned, we've been even more popular because the kids over there are really starved of big name groups. They love a good night out because it helps them forget the troubles.

Funnily enough, it all did a lot for our morale, too. We were playing to new audiences every night at first. They were giving us great receptions and we were earning money – and our own worries seemed to remain back in

Britain. I honestly believe these Irish visits helped to make The Rollers into what they are today.

I can confess now that at that time I was thinking to myself that maybe the management of the group had been really bad and I hadn't done everything possible for the group. I was beginning to get a bit disillusioned with the whole thing, especially when people in London had refused to listen to me. I was really weak that way. They all had their own ideas about The Bay City Rollers and nobody really wanted to listen to mine. Nobody had said to me: 'How do you see The Bay City Rollers?' I could have said quite a bit, but nobody wanted to listen.

But as the receptions in Ireland got wilder I thought to myself: 'Well, maybe there's hope yet.'

Anyway we returned to Scotland with a bit of money at last. Not enough to clear all our debts, but it was a start.

Everybody was full of hope for 'Saturday Night' when it came out in June, 1973. Everyone thought that this time we were really going to make it, but by now – believe it or not – I was beginning to have some trouble from the group.

They felt that I wasn't doing enough; that I wasn't fighting enough for their rights. Nobby felt he was writing a lot of good hit material. I disagreed with him, but I did think it would have been nice if we could have some of our own material on the 'B' sides of our records.

Anyway, the record came out and we continued playing all kinds of clubs; anything, in fact, that was acceptable and paid money. When it sunk in that 'Saturday Night' had failed as well, I thought: Well, that's that. The show's over. That's the finish.

To be fair, we held out hopes for that record for quite a while. It wasn't until the end of 1973 that we admitted it wasn't going to happen. In fact it had flopped by mid-

October but when you're so close to a record you keep hoping – and, after all, 'Keep On Dancing' had become a success after six months in the shops.

Eventually, I decided to go down to London alone to see Dick Leahy at Bell. The offices in those days were just off Berkeley Square, in Mayfair. They were very homely with a narrow entrance hall and a girl on the switchboard at the end of it. There was hardly a reception area to speak of – just a couch in the hall where you could wait. It was a small and friendly company with all these gold records on the entrance hall wall awarded to Bell artists like David Cassidy and Gary Glitter.

I was really nervous about the meeting that afternoon. As I was ushered into his room I said: 'Well ...' and waited for him to say: 'That's it then.' But he didn't. He said: 'We'll have another go with Bill Martin and Phil Coulter. But, remember, this will be it. They'll have to make it or break it on this one.'

So once again we were back in the studios. And once again we had a lot of arguments and hassles and things like that about what we'd play on the record. But finally we went ahead with the record, 'Remember'. Naturally we wanted the 'B' side, but that didn't happen and by this time I was having real trouble with Nobby. He was becoming neurotic about his songwriting and he argued that if he could get just one of his own records out it would mean everything. I could see his point, but we just couldn't do it like that at the time. I think Nobby must have met a girl by this time and that was the beginning of the end as far as he was concerned.

Nobby had really decided that he was going to leave. He didn't enjoy leaving Edinburgh; he'd been on the road a long time and I couldn't blame him. I was beginning to feel it, too. So were Alan and Derek.

I think we all felt the end was near. I was feeling depressed, but I always felt that The Rollers couldn't end just like that, after all we had been through together. We couldn't just give up. How could we have spent all those nights sleeping in the back of the van? Sleeping on the streets, cooking for ourselves? We'd fought together. We'd been injured in dance hall brawls. We'd done the lot. So I felt we couldn't give up that easily. I used to lie in bed at night for hours thinking: 'What will I ever do if it ends?' And other thoughts would race through my mind and stop me from sleeping. I'd think: 'I'm doomed. We've all had it.'

Then Derek came to see me and admitted he was thinking about leaving the group. He said he could get good regular work as a joiner and he wanted to look after his folks who were pretty hard up. I think that was one of the saddest nights of my life.

Derek came to my house early that evening to see me.

Because we had been together so long I immediately sensed something was wrong. I didn't even need him to tell me. He came into the room, sat down and then said very slowly and deliberately: 'I've been down to see about a job. I think I'm going to take it. That's it. Really. I think I've had it.'

You see, Derek and I were the only ones who really knew the true financial state of the group because he looked after the kitty. And by this time we were £7,000 in debt.

We talked on and on for hours. I kept saying we could still make it ... and then Derek actually burst into tears. I came close to tears myself because the group meant so much to us both and that night we could see no way out of our troubles. The only way was to have a hit – and we both admitted the likelihood of that happening overnight was unlikely.

I pleaded with Derek to hang on just a little bit longer and we even made plans to leave the country if everything went wrong. I said to him that if it didn't happen for us then I'd have to emigrate. I'd never be able to pay back £7,000 to anybody. Finally, Derek agreed to go back home and think it over.

That night I went to bed in the early hours. But I hardly slept a wink. I couldn't believe that The Bay City Rollers would be defeated just like that. The debt worried me, too, and I was worrying about Derek because I knew he might ring me later that day and say he was leaving.

A few hours later Derek did ring me.

Apparently he, too, had been awake most of the night, thinking about the problem. But he was ringing to tell me he had decided to go on. So now I had to think of yet another tactic to try to make the group succeed. I really felt sorry for Derek. Everything he had said about our financial state was true and I didn't blame him for wanting to get a regular job.

After a few days, I came up with a plan and called The Rollers around to my house one night. I told them I'd borrowed a few hundred pounds off my folks and had over 10,000 photographs of The Rollers printed. I'd also gone around Edinburgh buying up all those fan magazines listing the names and addresses of fans who wanted to get in touch with other people. That night we sat down and sent out nearly 10,000 Bay City Rollers pictures to these addresses with a note about a new record, saying: 'RE-MEMBER. Buy your copy now. Out on such and such a date.' Everybody thought I was crazy, but I put a lot of the success of that record down to that promotion.

We got some pretty weird letters back from some people saying things, such as: 'How dare you send a group photograph to me.' But to be fair there were very few of those.

'Remember' began to get moving, but I still felt changes would have to be made within the group, because I knew Nobby wanted to leave. I met Leslie in a rather strange way really. He'd been with this other group and he kept coming down to see me. In fact, at the slightest opportunity Leslie would always be there! When I knew for certain Nobby was leaving, I considered Leslie seriously as a replacement. And I came to the conclusion that he was just what we were looking for.

Nobby said he would stay with the group until Leslie had worked himself in, but suddenly he had a Christmas party or something to go to one night, and he didn't play. So Leslie was straight in on his own as lead singer. We were playing on the West Coast of Scotland, well away from where we lived, and we said to Leslie: 'Well, this is it. It looks like Nobby's left tonight.' I think, in fact, Nobby had wanted to get out as quickly as he could and there was poor Leslie left there. He hadn't even had time to learn his words. I'll never forget that because he had to sing his words off bits of paper stuck on cabinets at the side of the stage and all over the place. He had to keep leaning over to read them all the time. He did so well that I don't think anyone in the audience realized what was going on. The rest of the group were very grateful to him because Nobby had really dropped him in the deep end. Still, it's often good to start a new job that way because you either sink or swim. And Leslie, of course, has been swimming strongly ever since.

John Devine was still with the group then. But I knew he wanted to leave, too and I'd been keeping this from the rest of the boys. With Derek far from happy and Nobby walking out overnight, the morale of the group would have been very bad. And now we'd got Leslie I thought we should let him get properly worked in before any more changes were made. Leslie, in fact, was raring to go. He was fresh and it did the group good to have this new spirit around. The hard times we had had were beginning to show, but Leslie was a fighter and he gave us all strength, especially me because the conversation with Derek had affected me deeply and even I was starting to feel I had had enough.

It was just like when Eric joined the group. He'd given me strength at that time, but Eric was getting exhausted himself by now and wondering just what was going on. So here we were: Nobby, our main vocalist, had gone and we were genuinely in a bit of a state.

I must admit now that I hadn't got on well with Nobby. At first it was all right, but during the last twelve months it had been a real drag. He had got a bit old fashioned. So in came Leslie and after the hard work of getting all those photographs out all over the country I was on the phone to Bell Records every day, asking how many plays on the radio we'd had, and what our sales figures were.

You can imagine by now how desperate I was that 'Remember' would be a success. And, believe it or not, I used to sit and pray every night. I'm not a very religious person. I just used to sit there with my eyes closed and say: 'Please'. I don't think it was just for my sake either. It was just that I really wanted it to go because of Derek, Alan and Eric. I felt particularly sorry for Eric. I knew he would never pack it in and I was worried that he might have to go to London on his own with his guitar on his back and look for a job. That's all his life is: being in a group – and if he can take his guitar to bed with him then he's happy. Anyway, I think my prayers must have been answered because we started to sell 200 records a day. Then it went up to 300. And suddenly one week it started off with a fantastic figure of about nine hundred.

When I heard that figure I could hardly believe it. I thought: it's away. It has to be. The following day it was 1,400 and then off it went. We went in to what they call the 'breakers'. That's outside the top fifty but obviously one that's going to zoom in and up. Even on the figures that were being returned I thought we should have been in the charts. But we weren't and it wasn't long before all the old doubts started returning. I felt we could fall away at any moment without breaking into the charts. After all, that's the only thing that matters.

Then it happened. We became what is known as a star breaker. This is the name given to the record selling most outside the charts. One day Bell Records phoned me at home to tell me that Top of the Pops wanted to put The Rollers on because they were the star breaker.

It was two years since we had done Top of the Pops. Although we were advised to keep our smart cabaret look, I didn't want the group to appear in the kind of clothes they had worn for 'Keep On Dancing'.

People often ask me how The Bay City Rollers' dress style came about, so I'll explain.

All the time I was encouraging the boys to wear clothes their fans could identify with. We had tried to change our style while Nobby and John were in the group, but they liked the flared trousers.

It was Eric who started to change things. He said he was going to be an individual and create a new look. We decided to get the rest of the group to change.

Many of the kids in Scotland were wearing rather short trousers, so we exaggerated it, at Eric's suggestion. All the guys added something of their own and it began to be a trademark. Eventually we got designers in, and they too developed the ideas further.

However, it was on that edition of Top of the Pops that we introduced the new style.

Our money was drying up. We'd raked around, and I'd bled my mother to death. (I must say that if it had not been for my mother I'd have been bankrupt ages ago. She was unbelievable in her faith in everything The Rollers and I were doing.) Anyway, we realized we had to be inventive about our clothes without spending too much money. We knew the kids in Scotland were wearing these baggy trousers, so we got some and made them much shorter. Then we decided on the striped socks, and that was that.

Eric was in digs in Edinburgh, and we all piled around there. We all did our own tailoring. It was getting quite exciting. Leslie, of course, was especially keen on it all. We realized the whole thing was starting to build up again, and we had so much faith that it just carried us along. It did not seem to matter that we had no money and were in debt.

Driving down to London for that Top of the Pops show was like setting off for that Spanish holiday all over again. There was the same atmosphere of excitement. We were at Number 51 in the charts and everyone was joking as the van roared down the motorway. We looked back at all the hard times we'd shared and laughed at them. We were more than confident that Top of the Pops was going to do it for us.

By this time, 'Remember' was getting a lot of play on the air and the disc jockeys were starting to say it was going to be a hit, and all that sort of thing. But we still didn't have any money so we drove down overnight to save staying at a hotel in London. By the time we reached the BBC TV studios in Shepherd's Bush I think we really were even more excited than when we had left Edinburgh. For one thing we'd had no trouble with our van, and we felt that was a good omen in itself. When we stopped at the main gate of the TV Centre, a commissionaire came out of a little hut and peered into our van. He saw all the perky faces of The Rollers peering out from the back, and he laughed and wished us well as he let the gate up. In fact, the group always seem to get that reaction from people. I think it is because they are young and have all this enthusiasm for life that some older people seem to lose. Yes, everything seemed right for the great moment when we'd play 'Remember' on Top of the Pops. And to tell you the truth, even to this day none of the group can tell you who was on that show with us. As far as we were concerned, we were the only ones in the show.

Even when they were down and out, The Rollers have always been very professional. They always do what they have to do and then return to their dressing room whether it means waiting there for three or four hours. Other groups tend to hang about the bar, making themselves very accessible. I've always thought this takes something of the 'star' quality away from an act.

On the other hand, one has to have strong will power to sit in a dressing room for long periods. But on that particular day I don't think we really believed we were doing Top of the Pops. We almost had to keep pinching each other. We'd had a long journey down and, as Alan said, maybe we were still dreaming about it all.

Bell Records were very good to us that day. They kept bringing coffee and sandwiches in for us and we were very content.

Perhaps I ought to explain a little about Top of the Pops. You've probably seen it at home, but it's a very different thing being on it. A lot of people thought The Rollers were doing their record, but that wasn't so. We had to record a special track for the show and when we went on, the boys just sung. I've often heard it said: 'It's supposed to be live so why haven't they got leads plugged into their guitars?' But the groups who go on Top of the Pops record their number the day before, or on the morning of the show.

When a group arrive they are allocated a dressing room, and there is a loudspeaker system that calls them to the studio when they're needed. In the morning there is a band call. Everyone is brought down and the BBC band is there as well. Then they have a break for lunch and after that a dress rehearsal during which all the cameras are plotted. Finally all the kids are let in and the show goes on for real.

It's a very exciting show for a group to do because most of the groups who are in the Top Ten that week are there, and it's great seeing a lot of people you may just have read about or heard on the radio.

The kids that night showed quite a bit of interest in The Rollers even though we weren't in the charts at the time. And it was no doubt due to the startling new clothes the boys were wearing, which was astonishing really when you remember they had been born out of economic necessity. The trousers Eric wore that night had been bought from an Army surplus store for just two pounds. And all he did was sew a bit of tartan around the top part. He actually sewed it himself – he's clever like that. Leslie decided he would wear boots and I think they were the dearest thing we bought. Leslie's dad took his trousers up for him. We had gone into all these ex-Army and Navy stores looking for stuff we could adapt and we bought V-neck sweaters for £3 and white shirts. We sewed things on these as well. If you worked out what the group paid for their gear on Top of the Pops that night then I'd say it was less than £10. The only things that were a bit dear were the shoes but we borrowed some money from Bell Records for these. I think they were glad to give us some money at this time because they also felt we were about to burst on the scene.

When the show was over everyone went up to the bar, but we drove straight back to Scotland. It's very nice meeting people, but if you don't drink alcohol, why go to a bar? The Rollers are their own company. Wherever we travel, we stop and have a milk or something, but never ever go into pubs.

Things, financially, were still bad. We had only two jobs that week, both in Scotland. We had spread our wings slightly over England, Wales and Ireland, but now we had retreated to Scotland because of our financial difficulties. So we drove back after Top of the Pops to do these two shows – and to watch the show on TV the next night.

We watched it in Eric's flat. I say a flat, but it was actually just one room. He didn't have a colour TV so we watched it in black and white. Naturally, we were very excited watching ourselves on a big show like that for only the second time. After that appearance, our record went higher and higher up the charts. We started selling 5,000 a day and at last we were able to go out on the road for a bit more money once again.

Now we were able to demand £200 a night, which lifted the morale of the group.

Everything, for once, seemed to be working well, so I decided to have a long talk with John to see what he really wanted to do. I'd already seen this young guy called Woody playing with a group called Kip in Edinburgh and I knew that if ever we needed another replacement he would be right for the job.

John had said he wanted to leave when Nobby went but he was always a very fair person and he said he would stay on until I felt times were easier. When 'Remember' became a success I thought John might have changed his mind about leaving, but when I asked him he said he felt that he wasn't really meant for the music business. He also felt that the type of life did not suit him. But he made it clear that he wanted to leave the group as a friend.

To be honest, I'd actually asked Woody before 'Remember' was made and there was a time when it was going up the charts that I thought I may have put myself in an awkward situation. I'd almost promised Woody a job you see, but if John was going to stay, there wouldn't be any job for Woody. Still, everything sorted itself out: John knew I'd sounded out Woody and was quite happy to go. So all I had to do now was tell the rest of the group.

I told Eric first. He was shocked at the thought of John leaving because they had always got on very well. But he liked the idea of Woody coming in because he'd seen Woody playing with Kip.

I chose Woody because he was young. He had visited me and phoned me up regularly to see what was happening. And I really saw him as a Roller.

This might prompt you to ask what is the ideal Roller? Well, he would be young, fresh-faced, full of energy, well mannered – and in Woody's case he would have to be good on guitar. Which he was. He was always interested in writing songs, too. Before he joined The Rollers, he would phone up and say: 'I've written this song. I want you to listen to it.' And then he would sing it over the telephone. His songs were all right at that time, but I didn't think they were Number One material. Mind you, I don't think that even Paul McCartney or John Lennon could have done better when they were sixteen, which was Woody's age at the time. What I particularly liked about Woody was his enthusiasm. He was determined to be a Roller and was on the phone every night, asking me what the position was. He even started cutting his hair in the 'tufty' style and getting his 'Roller' clothes together.

The rest of the group were shocked about John, but they were dead keen on Woody as a person because of his determination to become a Roller.

Meanwhile, John had met a very nice girl and really wanted to settle down. He had been on the road and kicked about with the rest of us for quite a long time and in the end he wasn't really interested in show business.

I've often been accused of never letting The Rollers meet girls – but that's rubbish. I don't run their lives, they can have girlfriends anytime. In Scotland they need never come around to see me. I certainly don't know where they go to at nights and I don't mind, as long as they behave themselves and treat people right. I think most of their off-duty time is spent writing songs. I know that Eric, Woody and Leslie are always sitting around writing songs and arranging them. They've got tape recorders and things like that and Leslie will turn up at my place at two in the morning after they've written a song and he'll just say: 'You ought to hear this song – it's fantastic.' And he'll play it back to me on his recording machine.

Sometimes I've heard the sound of small stones hitting my bedroom window and it's Leslie sitting in his car outside waiting to be let in so that he can have a chat.

When you're on the road all the time, of course, it's almost impossible to meet girls. After driving perhaps 200 miles in a day we'll only have time to check into a hotel and have dinner before it's time to do a concert. We won't finish until nearly midnight, so you can see there's not much time to meet girls – unless one is talking about inviting them back to the hotel rooms. And we're not at all interested in that. I'm not saying that so people will think what a lovely clean image The Rollers have. A lot of nonsense has been written about what pop groups get up to. People tend to think nowadays that just because you're in a group, you're likely to have ten girls in your bedroom. But I maintain that it's quite normal for a group such as The Rollers to travel up and down the country without dragging girls into their rooms every night. I'm not saying that the boys will always stay the way they are now, but that sort of thing certainly doesn't happen at the moment. They just do not seem to be interested.

One thing they do, though, is consult me about their problems. Being young they do have problems just like everyone else. When a group becomes famous, people tend to forget they are human. It is their singing and musical ability that has made them different from the rest of their generation, but when they come off stage and relax they suffer from the same sort of problems that affect other young people.

For example, would you believe Woody worries a lot about his spots? I never notice them, and he says I never notice them because I'm not a girl. But I've told him that if girls really like him they won't care about his spots. And to tell you the truth I think he imagines there are many more spots than there actually are.

Leslie is very critical of himself, too. He'll worry about how his hair is, and he'll always come up to me when the group are to go on TV and say: 'Do I look all right? Is everything OK?' I enjoy that actually. I feel quite honoured. He'll say: 'How's my make-up?' The Rollers don't wear make-up in the sense that a lot of people think they wear make-up. They only really wear it for television. And you have to be careful how you are made up because sometimes it can look too heavy. That's why Leslie always asks my advice about that.

The boys wear a small amount of make-up when they're on stage live. They sometimes have just that bit of colour, like a dab on the face with a sponge and stuff called pan-stick, but that's all. They don't spend three hours doing their eyes up, or anything like that. It's just make-up for the lights really because strong lighting makes one look very pale. I don't think The Rollers have to enhance themselves any other way than that.

As for Derek, he's not the sort of guy who will discuss a problem with anyone. He keeps everything to himself. I never like using the words 'very deep' because I think that sounds bad and there's nothing bad about Derek. I just think he never likes to bother anybody. But I can always tell if something is bothering him and I'll say: 'Is everything all right?' Then he'll probably talk about it. The trouble is that he builds things up within himself. Take those debts, for example. I'm a bit like Leslie – I get my head down and tackle the problem in a tough way. I like a good old fight. But Derek's very careful. He likes to plan everything out, and he wouldn't like to get into any more debt without knowing all about it. There would have to be some plan made there and then to clear that debt. He was also very worried about his mother for quite a long time. His mother had a long illness. She suffered from chronic bronchitis and I think when we were on the road many times his mother was quite ill. Derek worried secretly a lot about that. I think he would take everything into himself and it would suddenly build up and as a result he would get really ill; really upset.

While Leslie will always come to me with a problem, Derek certainly won't. But I can always tell when something's worrying him.

He is asthmatic, and I'd say it's nervous. He is seeing a specialist, and we hope he will be cured. It seems to be working out well, because he hasn't had a recurrence of the kind of attack he suffered in 1974.

We're glad we've got the money now to do something like sending him to a specialist.

Now his brother Alan is very different. He worries too, but I find he is the most mature member of The Rollers. I can have a sensible conversation with Alan. He's the sort of guy who has no problems, and even if he did he's not the type who would see it as a problem. If he had a pimple somewhere or other he wouldn't think it a problem, like Woody. He'd just put a patch on it and wait for it to clear up.

Then there's Eric. Believe it or not, he's very nervous.

If you hear him speak then you might notice it, because sometimes he'll sort of stutter or stammer over a word. We're very close, although he can be a bit of a rebel with me at times. Sometimes he doesn't accept what I say, but we always end up doing what I say in the end. I think he's got to show that he can be a little bit independent. And I always find with Eric that he is the one who is always worried about the group breaking up. I think this causes him to be nervous. He'll sit with a pen and scribble away on pieces of paper and things like that just to relieve the nerves, I suppose. Recently, though, his nerves have been all right. We have small tiffs, but never what you'd call an argument. I don't want to give the impression that Eric and I are always fighting, because that is not true. We understand each other very well. You see, with him there's no compromise. It's either one way or the other.

Let me give you an example. I've always encouraged Eric to write songs and after working on a number, for say, three weeks, he'll come to me and say : 'What do you think?' If I say : 'Well, really, Eric I don't like it. There's just something missing,' he's just as likely to snap : 'Oh hell, right, fine, I'm not going to write again.' He certainly wouldn't sit down calmly and say : 'Well, I'll go away and write another one.'

This sort of thing has happened at the studios. The boys refuse to let me hear the song until it is finished. They'll keep me sitting outside the studio for an hour or more, then they'll pop their heads round the corner and chorus : 'You can't come in now. You can't come in now.' Then when I finally go in and say I don't like it, Eric's likely to go into a huff and say he won't write any more. So there you are. But the point I'm making is that Eric is very highly strung and a very creative person.

Sometimes I wish more of the group would be interested in the business side of things and not just the creative side. I'd certainly value their criticism. Maybe this may happen as they get a little older. At the moment, money doesn't seem to bother them very much. They just like doing what they're doing. In 1975 each Roller has been getting £35 to

£40 pocket money a week. In addition, money is drafted into their accounts every year, and they've got their own bank accounts. So if we do a tour and draw £50,000 about £8,000 will go into each of The Rollers's own account. But, as I said, they don't seem to worry. Money just doesn't seem to bother them, which, in itself, is quite strange.

But let's go back to when everything was beginning to happen with 'Remember' getting into the charts. Woody had joined us and John Devine had left, which meant that Woody had to learn the words of a chart hit. Isn't that incredible? Here we were with a chart hit and two members of the original group missing. It worried me a lot at the time, but when Woody joined the group The Rollers just became more popular than ever.

The popularity that was starting to happen seemed endless. We were even being accepted in the same ballrooms whose audiences before had been lukewarm. The crowds were getting really enthusiastic and it was quite enjoyable because every time The Rollers went on stage now we had two hit numbers – 'Keep on Dancing' and 'Remember' – and there were even the odd screams. The whole ballroom audience used to stop, whatever they were doing, and just stand and watch the group playing. At first this was quite frightening. Certainly it was very different from the early days. The days seemed to go very quickly then. In no time at all we'd performed 'Remember' on four Top of the Pops and then we were asked to appear on other shows like '45' and Lift Off in Manchester. Back in London we got The Basil Brush Show. It all seemed to be happening, yet there was still that nagging feeling at the back of my mind that it might all suddenly stop again.

Television is very important to a group – especially a new group like The Rollers – because you just can't get around to enough people by playing ballrooms. You need that networked exposure all over Britain at the one time, or even local television, which will cover the whole of one certain area. It is because of this that I think the TV situation in this country at the moment is very sad, as far as the BBC is concerned. You can't get on Top of the Pops unless you have a hit single – yet how can you get a hit single without exposure? It's the same with BBC radio. There's a panel of five people who choose which records are to be played on Radio One and I think because of this system there is a lot of stifled talent in this country.

Looking back, I think it's a miracle that The Bay City Rollers got on Top of the Pops as a breaker. They have dropped that system. Nowadays, I think you've got to actually be in the Top 50 before you get on. I honestly believe we got on because Bell Records and ourselves pestered them so much they thought: 'God, let's have this group on.' They knew we'd been going for about five years.

Still, success had started to come at last and it's only from this standpoint that one can comment on such matters. Otherwise it would seem too much like sour grapes.

We were now up to £300 a night. Derek had started smiling again, because we were at last able to start repaying money we owed. And I must say that it was partly due to his strict budgeting that this was possible. Despite our sudden success we were still living off £7 a week each, and I was delighted about the debt situation. It was something that at times I had thought almost impossible! At last I could actually go into the bank and face the bank manager!

But one record doesn't make a successful pop group and I still had a nagging feeling that it might all be another 'Keep On Dancing'. Our next record took on even more importance than 'Remember'. The success of 'Remember' had kept the group alive. If it had not succeeded, let's face it, I think that might have been that. But now 'Remember' had to be followed by another hit or we'd be right back where we'd started. And I really don't think we could have faced that again despite the new blood and energy of Leslie and Woody. The battle for success takes a lot out of one both mentally and physically, and when it depends on where your record is in the charts it can be even worse.

Anyway, Bill Martin and Phil Coulter came up with the record to follow 'Remember'. It was called 'Shang-a-Lang' and it was recorded under very different circumstances compared with the past. For a start, we were able to afford a car to take us to the recording studios and we stayed in a very pleasant hotel, the Royal Norfolk Hotel, near Paddington Station. We could afford decent meals and have a warm night's sleep in fresh linen every night. We still shared rooms of course, as we've always done. This puzzles some hotels sometimes. They think we're trying to save on the bills, but it's not true.

Well, with 'Shang-a-Lang' I didn't even have time to pray as I had done with 'Remember'. The new single shot straight into the charts and it just seemed that all the success we'd had with 'Remember' continued without a break. In no time at all, we were back on Top of the Pops and all the other shows.

It had now become obvious to everyone in the music industry that The Rollers had arrived. And, if anything, the crowds at the ballrooms got even bigger. And almost to celebrate the fact, we bought a new van for equipment, much to the delight of Jake, our faithful roadie, who has put up with a lot over the period he's been with The Rollers.

With this new found popularity we were now going to learn about the physical side of success. Not only does it tend to wear you out but the enthusiasm of the fans knows no bounds. Everyone just wants to touch one of The Rollers or ask for an autograph as they are leaving a venue. And now life was becoming very difficult for the first time.

You must remember that almost as soon as we'd had a success with 'Remember', then 'Shang-a-Lang', The Rollers brought out 'Summer' and the success of this really fuelled the fire of the fan mania. We were literally getting pulled to pieces and many a night we'd get back to the hotel and Alan, Derek, Leslie, Woody or Eric would be black and blue with bruises where fans had grabbed at them.

Things were getting so difficult that I felt that our days of playing ballrooms were coming to an end, but the trouble was no one would believe how successful The Rollers were until they had seen the fans in action themselves. I would go in and say to a ballroom manager: 'There will be a bit of a riot.' They would reply confidently: 'Oh we've had lots of groups here. It'll be alright.'

They wouldn't understand that The Rollers were a very different proposition now to any other group that had been around in Britain for years. And, of course, by the time the boys had got halfway through their act the ballroom manager would have turned white.

One particular ballroom – in Shrewsbury, I think – didn't have any barriers. I told the manager they would be needed, but he said they wouldn't. I said: 'I've heard that from 1,000 other managers, but I warn you you'll need barriers.' Like all the rest he blurted out a list of groups and stars which had appeared there; 'I've had Suzi Quatro here. We've had Slade, we've had them all here.' I couldn't persuade him and I thought to myself that we couldn't refuse to go on because of all the kids in the hall, and hundreds queueing outside.

I have never refused to let The Rollers go on, we're very close to our audience and we'd never let them down. We've always thought: Why should they suffer because of older people who don't understand what's going on? So we went on stage in Shrewsbury.

And it was terrible. From the first note The Rollers played, youngsters were fainting and screaming. The manager started to panic and ordered adults from behind the coffee bar to get down to the front of the stage. I think we lasted 35 minutes before the manager pleaded with me to get the boys off the stage. Well, I did take them off, but that didn't stop the scenes. We all finally ended up trapped in the manager's office with fans screaming and hammering on the door. Eventually the police arrived. As they battled their way through to the office, the manager turned to me and said: 'I've never seen anything like it in my whole life.' And he kept muttering it to himself until the police got us out. And that was the story from hall to hall.

When we played at Sunderland Locarno it was like a football match outside. There were queues all the way down the street, like a big game. Once again I said to the manager of the hall that I hoped the barriers would be all right. He looked at me and said, 'Look here, son, I've had Led Zeppelin, Rod Stewart and The Faces here. I know what to do.'

I said, 'I can't argue about that. I think Led Zeppelin's fantastic. But they draw a different type of audience.'

It was at this point that I decided we'd had enough hassles. I was getting very frustrated going around these halls, listening to managers telling me this and me that and I decided that from then on we'd do only concerts, where we could keep a control on the audience. At our concerts the audience is seated, and the stage is well raised, with maybe an orchestra pit separating it from the audience.

The security is in the hands of the people presenting the group, which cuts down on the risk of anyone being hurt.

We had a few dates to complete after playing Sunderland and at one of them in Margate I saw a lot of kids being hurt. I'd had the usual conversation with the manager when we arrived about security – or rather lack of it, but he obviously thought: 'It's only The Bay City Rollers again.' You see we'd appeared there about three years before and times were very different. Now there was a massive queue outside an hour or so before the show and at the sight of it the manager panicked. He went to the local fairground and picked up about fifteen thugs and plonked them along the front of the stage. Soon after The Rollers started playing, I saw kids kicked and punched some punched in the mouth. It was the most disgusting gig I've ever been to in my life. I'm not saying it was the manager's fault, but just that people kept under-rating the effect The Rollers had on their audience. And I hated violence.

Anyway we decided to stop touring the halls, and because of our sudden success it was to be the most different and enjoyable break any of us had ever experienced.

'SUMMER LOVE SENSATION'

It all started at my local travel agent in Edinburgh.

I went down there one morning and asked him where would be the sunniest place in the world at the moment. He was a bit surprised at first because he remembered the time we had to hitch-hike all the way from Spain because we had no money. It was the wrong time of the year for Spanish sunshine, so he thought for a while, then said: 'There's only one place I can recommend if you want it really hot – and that is Jamaica.'

Imagine the thought of flying off to Jamaica, even a year or so before we'd have just laughed among ourselves. Alan would have cracked a whole lot of Jamaican jokes and that would have been that.

But this was reality. We could actually afford to take a real break, and so we decided to go to Montego Bay. Not everyone came with me to Jamaica. Eric said he wanted a complete rest away from everything so that he could spend some time writing. So he plumped for – would you believe it? – a health farm. We booked him into the best one we could find in the South of England.

Leslie didn't come either. The mental strain had been unbelievable and he felt that he just wanted to get away with his family. His mother had never had a holiday and he decided to take her to the South of France. There had been other strains for other members of the group. While 'Shang-a-Lang' was actually rising in the charts in the Spring of 1973 the Longmuirs' mother died, and this affected both Alan and Derek very much.

She had been ill for many years with chronic bronchitis, and she had a bad heart as well. Her death had in fact affected the whole group and it's something I'll never forget. The thing I'll always admire Derek and Alan for was that the day after she died we flew to London to do Top of the Pops. I remember speaking to them and I said that we'd only do the programme if they really wanted to. They both came to me and told me that they would do the show because that was what their mother would have wished. I thought it was very brave of them because she meant so much to them, and although she had been ill all this time her death still came as a very deep shock to them.

In fact the night before we flew down to do the show Derek was sharing a room with Woody and the next day he told me that he was lying in bed thinking and couldn't get to sleep. Woody was asleep and Derek was crying because he kept thinking about his mother. Suddenly, he told me, he had this strange feeling. He felt that somebody was leaning over him, and it was as though someone had touched him. When he turned around, he claimed he saw something disappearing into the ground. After that he felt a bit better, and much more at ease. He reckons it was his mother who was in the hotel and she'd just come along to comfort him, and he believed he was doing the right thing by doing Top of the Pops.

After we did the show we went back to Scotland for the funeral. We asked all the fans to stay away, and they did. It was all very sad, and Alan and Derek were heartbroken. Their mother was a very nice lady. The Longmuirs were never a very wealthy family, and although they didn't live in an expensive house Mrs. Longmuir always kept the home spotless. She always cooked the family nice meals and looked after her sons and daughters very well.

A few weeks later Derek collapsed while he was at home from a particularly bad asthmatic attack. I've no doubt at all that the main reason for this was his mother's death.

Derek was very close to his mother and he shows his emotions. I sometimes worry about Alan because I don't think he shows his emotions. I think Alan shows a face. Maybe more people were inclined to feel sorry for Derek because he does show his emotions, and they're inclined to forget about Alan. I felt sorry for Alan because I realized he was being strong about the whole thing.

Anyway when it came to us all going on holiday Alan took his dad and they went to Spain. Woody, Derek, and I went to Jamaica.

As we climbed higher and higher above London Airport in a Jumbo jet, Woody, Derek and me grinned at each other, as much to give each other confidence as anything.

I don't think anyone, if they're being really honest, enjoys flying, especially the take-off when you seem to be going up like a rocket. Still, after travelling all those thousands of miles in old vans this was real luxury and soon the great jet had levelled out, and we could see the sun through the window sparkling on the tops of the clouds beneath us, which now seemed like snow-covered mountains.

We unfastened our seat belts and were soon tucking into the first meal of our holiday served by the very beautiful and pleasant stewardesses. All the time the three of us kept thinking back to the first holiday in Spain and how very different things were now.

There are all sorts of advantages to flying, not least the fact that you can watch a movie as you're flying through the air at several hundred miles per hour. A screen is lowered at the front of the cabin and you plug in an ear-piece to get the sounds.

Jamaica was everything we'd dreamed about. We stayed at the Chatham Beach Hotel, in Montego Bay and every day was blue skies, hot sun, and white sandy beaches.

That first morning, after we'd all had a good sleep we almost didn't know what to do with ourselves. When you've been as busy as The Rollers had been it takes some time to unwind. But soon Woody, Derek and I were learning how to scuba dive. This is underwater swimming with glass goggles on so that you can see the bottom of the sea and the multi-coloured fish swimming all around. The water out there is so clear that in fact you can see everything that is going on underneath the surface.

At night we used to sit on the hotel verandah and eat our meals in the warmth of the evening. They go in for a lot of fish-type dishes out there, which both Woody and Derek liked very much. It made a great change from the usual fish and chips we'd been eating at motorway cafes all those years. Now our fish was served on great big plates with all the trimmings or cut up and served in little shells covered with cream, cheese and other sorts of sauces.

The great thing was that it was all so different to what we'd been going through recently in Britain. After six months of being recognized in the street we could wander anywhere without anyone bothering us. We also met a lot of nice people and at first I'll admit we got a few old fashioned looks from the locals because both Woody and Derek wore their usual Rollers outfits even out there on holiday. Actually, in a hot sunny climate like Jamaica it was quite practical having your trousers ending quite high up your legs and just tee shirts above them.

Both Woody and Derek suffered a bit from the sun. They were so pleased to be on holiday that they couldn't spend long enough on the beach at first. They both went pink and suffered a bit of sunburn, so for a few days they had to take it easy.

By the end of the holiday though, they had both turned a superb golden brown. They spent a lot of time swimming, running up and down the beach and just sleeping in the sun. The really odd thing was that we got up so early every morning. Of course, when you're a rock group you tend to have to get up later in the day because your work is at night and you need your sleep just like anybody else. But Woody and Derek were up every day at half past seven. They just didn't want to waste a minute of the sunshine, and it also meant that they were in bed every night pretty early as well, worn out. They never went out and tried the night life. In fact, I was the one who went to a discotheque one or two nights. And in the morning the two boys would wake up and ask: 'What time did you get in last night?'

This was the first time The Rollers had ever been apart and it wasn't long before we were called to the telephone. Eric was phoning from the health farm in England. That phone call must have cost him pounds because he spoke to Woody, Derek and then me. I had my birthday when I was out there and Eric, Leslie and Alan sent me telegrams from the different holiday places they were in which touched me very much. But that is the way it has always been with The Rollers. We're a very close group, we have suffered so much it has brought us close together. Those birthday telegrams are a good example of everyone keeping in touch even though we'd never said anything to each other when we'd all set off in different directions.

Woody, Derek and I had been in Jamaica about nine days when suddenly one morning there was another phone call. This time it was Bell Records. 'Summer Love Sensation' had gone into the charts at number four and they wanted us back in London to do Top of the Pops.

We thought we would rather stay here lazing in the sun than jet back to London to appear on television. Once again our minds went back to when we had to battle to get on that same show. Now here we were lazing our days away in Jamaica, and Top of the Pops were contacting us to come back and do their show. It certainly can be a crazy world at times.

Of course, we had to go back and do our duty. That's the way it is with The Rollers. Work always comes before pleasure. In a way the boys were eager to get cracking again because this time we knew that at last we were really a success. Our latest record was blasting its way straight into the charts without hanging about for months.

Sadly the three of us packed our cases and got a cab to the airport. It had been a great break and Woody and Derek had relaxed and got really healthy again. But before we finally left Jamaica we went on a quick shopping expedition to buy presents for the rest of the group. We took Alan, Leslie and Eric back Jamaican knives. Alan, Eric and Leslie brought back presents for us as well, and we had a great reunion at a hotel in London to compare tans and experiences. Eric was a bit envious, I think, but he looked really well and had enjoyed himself. Leslie and Alan also had great tans and we all agreed it had been a good thing for us to have a rest. But it was also agreed that as far as The Rollers were concerned Top of the Pops was one of the most enjoyable ones they had done because they were fresh and full of vitality. They really looked good with their dark brown skins contrasting with their white trousers and tee shirts.

In fact it was a very special edition of Top of the Pops. It was hosted by The Osmonds who had been in London presenting a nightly live TV show on the BBC for a week.

Their shows had been immensely poplar, so that particular Thursday even more people than usual were watching, and the show went out live rather than being recorded the day before, as usually happens.

There was a real air of excitement as The Rollers drove up to the TV Theatre on Shepherds Bush Green from where the show was being done for that week only. In no time at all The Osmonds were chatting away to The Rollers. Donny Osmond was especially fascinated by the use of tartan on the boys outfits. Little Jimmy was there too, and spoke to Alan and Derek. The lovely Marie Osmond made all the boys' hearts miss a beat I think. Alan and Eric were in deep conversation with Wayne and Merrill Osmond, and it really seemed that we could not have staged a better 'Welcome back' to Britain. They were fascinated by our Scots accents. Like The Rollers they don't drink, so we were able to share a soft drink together and for once not feel out of things.

Outside the TV Theatre the scenes were incredible. There were literally thousands of girls. You could even hear their screams from inside the dressing rooms. I think that is one of the happiest shows we've ever worked on.

After the show they wished us all the best for the future. Everyone was very pleased with The Rollers' performance. As you can imagine it was not one of the easiest shows to play because of the immense popularity of The Osmonds themselves. I think this experience made us all the more sympathetic when we appeared on a show at London Weekend TV directed by Mike Mansfield in January of 1975. We followed another Scots artist, Maggie Bell, who is a very dear person, but I'm afraid we had to enter the studio while she was still singing and all the audience screamed for The Rollers.

When groups like The Rollers and The Osmonds are

around I'm afraid that sort of thing is bound to happen, however much we try not to upset other people's performances. Anyway, the next day the boys sent Maggie a bottle of champagne and a large bunch of flowers just to let her know we liked her.

Now our popularity really began to escalate and it became impossible for us to do anything that we had taken for granted before. Everyone wanted to write about the group too. I should explain to everyone reading this book that they should not believe everything they read in the press. They should take a lot of it with a pinch of salt. We have had girls writing to us saying that they are going to commit suicide because they have read somewhere that Eric is going around with a girl named Jenny. Stories like that are made up by people who can't get to talk to the group in person. The trouble is that when they print something like that without checking their facts, they don't realize the serious consequences it can cause.

I can assure everyone that no member of The Rollers has a steady girlfriend. No doubt some day they will, indeed I hope they will. One day I'd love to go to a wedding involving one of The Rollers. I'd like to see them all happily married eventually, but that would be sometime in the future. Their schedule at present is so full that they just don't have time to get to know any girls.

I'll give you an example of a typical schedule in a day in the life of a Bay City Roller in February 1975.

I am sitting in our hotel just off a motorway near London. I'm sharing a room with Woody, who is in the bathroom washing his hair. It is eleven o'clock and he has just woken up because we didn't get back from recording our latest album up in Chipping Norton, Oxfordshire, until the early hours of this morning.

Today is meant to be what we call a rest day. That

means the group will not be in the studio, which is why they are back in this hotel to relax over the weekend.

The phone has already started to ring with requests for us to do this and that.

I've also made my weekly call to my mother to get all the details about the fan club. The report from up there in Prestonpans is that there are 11,000 letters a day coming in.

Another man has rung to say he is bringing a car over for us to look at. We've decided among ourselves that we should get a big American car so that we can all travel in comfort together.

We've just heard that we are to be awarded a Carl Alan Award for the best group of the year, which means being presented to Princess Anne, so I've arranged for our tailor to come to the hotel later this morning for fittings and to discuss ideas about the clothes the group should wear for that very important occasion.

Then there are discussions due to take place involving concessions. This covers all the posters and other merchandising bearing The Rollers' name. We are aware of all sorts of unauthorized people pushing out stuff to the fans which we do not think is up to our high standards. The point of getting one person to run all this part of our organization is to give the fans a square deal. This is something The Rollers have always been very aware of. But when success happens suddenly you are just not geared up to deal with all these problems. However, everything is getting sorted out now and there will soon be very good Rollers watches, scarves, caps, socks, tee shirts and other goods on sale which will also earn some money for the group.

Woody has just finished washing his hair and is now rummaging around for the hair dryer. He is wearing his red trousers this morning, and as he dries his hair he is reading a Scottish newspaper that has put the group on their cover and carried the profile of them over on to page two. For us, coming from Scotland, this is really wonderful and beyond our wildest dreams. There is a poster lying on my bed for Woody to sign, left there by the girls who work at the hotel. They are very good and haven't bothered the boys at all so I'll see to it that the poster gets signed. As you'll have gathered by now our lives are not our own.

It's not that we don't love all this success – we certainly do – but I just want to show you that success is not all roses and autographs.

Excuse me while I just pop into the corridor to knock on the other doors just to check that everyone is up.

Yes, they're all getting up, although in Leslie's case a bit slowly this morning. Well you can't blame them because they've been working really hard this past week, going into the studios at mid-day and then working through until the early hours of the morning. Phil Wainman, their new producer, forbade me to take the film projector up to Chipping Norton because he said when they'd finished work they should go straight to sleep. But when they arrived back in the early hours of this morning they persuaded me to put a film on the projector, which I did so they didn't go to bed for another two hours. Very naughty of them, but you can't blame them and they have worked very well this week.

I've just heard on the phone that our accountant wants to see us all for an hour or so this afternoon, and I've promised my partner Barry Perkins that we'll all go over and attend the christening of his daughter. And when I was on the phone to my mother she asked me whether I'll be wearing a suit and tie, because she knows I like to just go around very casually dressed. In fact when I'm in a hotel

I never wear shoes or socks, I just like the freedom not wearing shoes gives me.

In no time at all the tailors are knocking on my door, and Woody has to put a tee shirt on. I assemble the group in Derek's bedroom, which he is sharing with Eric. Everyone has lots of ideas of what they want to wear and the young designers also brought plenty of ideas with them.

I return to my room because the phone never seems to stop ringing. It's funny how, with us being away all week, people suddenly realize they can get at us again.

Suddenly Leslie bursts into the room in a very natty half-finished outfit. It's all white as usual but has this blue motif down the sides and on the jacket. For once it isn't tartan but Leslie likes it very much and so do I. I tell him so and he is pleased, because he's always a bit uncertain about these things.

The trousers are not finished yet and will need taking up, but I like the whole idea of the outfit. Leslie looks good in it, so we decided that is how Princess Anne will see him. The Carl Alan Awards usually demand evening dress but I've decided – with the boys' backing – that they would look wrong in that, and they should appear in what they wear normally. I am sure Princess Anne will enjoy seeing them like that anyway.

One by one the group come parading into my room to see what I think of their outfits. I think they are all splendid.

Next there is a tap on my ground floor French window. It is the man about the car. As our tailors leave, the boys all change back into their other outfits and set off with me for a trial drive in the large white American car. Leslie is the great car expert so we're looking to him to tell us all about it.

When we get back from a short spin around the locality

Leslie is busy lifting up the bonnet and looking into the engine. He dives into the hotel to get something so that he can lie under the car and look into it from there. He's very thorough, and he doesn't feel we should buy this one. We don't.

Later we did buy a large American car with Leslie's approval. But his knowledge of these matters never ceases to astound me.

As you see, we make all decisions together, which is why I had to get them all up this morning. There would never be a situation with The Rollers where one of them would not be with the others. Everyone goes out in the car because finally everyone is going to ride in it when we're going to gigs. This way we have no disagreements and everyone knows that they have an equal say.

Often we're accused of being anti-social, of not welcoming other people, of not joining in. I would say that The Rollers are anti-social because they've come across so many people who want to swindle them. It's surprising once you get a bit of money, how many new friends you find yourself with – friends you didn't have when you were unsuccessful.

They don't really mix very well. We never go to parties. And this is not a case of Tam Paton not allowing them to go, which some newspapers have accused me of. The fact is that they just don't have the time. If you are out at parties all night then it affects your work in the end, especially if you have to work a schedule like ours.

Back to the schedule. By now it is about lunchtime, and we don't really feel like lunch just yet, so Woody rings up room service and orders a glass of milk and a selection of sandwiches. I usually have a cup of hot chocolate for breakfast and a bread roll with butter.

One good thing about the tailors coming is that for some

reason or other they brought a white shirt with them that fits me perfectly, so I won't let my mother down at the christening this afternoon. It looks really good with a freshly pressed light blue suit I've got, and I'm actually at this moment knotting a tie around my neck, a thing almost unseen until today. Woody gets a bit anxious at this point because I tell him there might be photographers at the christening, and he's worried about his spots. But I soon tell him nobody will notice them, and his hair looks great as it always does when it's just washed.

Leslie keeps on dashing in and out like a big puppy. You certainly wouldn't have thought he'd been working the hours he has this week. His energy seems boundless. He always seems to have a question for me to answer. Right now the problem is who has taken the Scottish paper that Woody was reading on his bed. It had only been lent to us by someone staying in the hotel. It is eventually found quite safe in Derek's room.

Next there are the cans of films to be sorted through. Some of them have to be sent back tomorrow so that we can hire some more. We usually keep a stock of seven or eight films at a time, and they really have proved the best investment we've made. When you get back in the early hours of the morning either from the recording studios or a concert you don't want to go to bed immediately. You have to have a period of unwinding.

Watching a film for an hour or so gets you ready for a good night's sleep. They are not too expensive to hire, and it means you can always see the film you want to see.

Before we set off to the christening I have to do another general round up of the rooms to get the boys all out together on time. By now some of them are watching their colour TVs, or making calls home on the phone, or hastily having breakfast. The advantage of staying in good hotels is that you can get all your meals delivered to your rooms. At this one you can also have a swim and after that a sauna bath.

This is the perfect combination to freshen you up and keep your body well-tuned. After the comparative chill of the swimming pool, you enter the wood-lined sauna room which gives out dry heat from a charcoal burner. It gets so hot you think your hair is going to catch fire, but it rids your body of all the unwanted things that accumulate in a busy life.

Before we leave there's yet another phone call, this time from Bell Records. They are putting the finishing touches to a visit we've promised to make to a hospital tomorrow to see one of our fans who was run over just before Christmas. Even as we're going to the door the phone rings again. This time it remains unanswered.

We have to be very careful about leaving the hotel. We've been here off and on for about a month now and the fans haven't really discovered us. I've had to tell Jake to drive the van straight back into London because it's an instant giveaway with all the group's names scrawled time and time across it. I know that's what fans like to do, to show their faith to a group, but believe you me, it sets us back at least £1,000 when it comes to respraying the van. It all has to be scraped down before it is repainted.

But because you use nail-files and other sharp objects to scratch the boys names on the van the metal is affected, and so it costs us a lot more. So remember that, the next time you scrawl something on a group's van!

'ALL OF ME LOVES ALL OF YOU'

We're not going to buy a new van just yet because Jake reports that this one is doing very well, but we have finally bought a large American car for the group to travel in together. Leslie had already turned down several more cars on my behalf when one day as we were driving in a limousine into London, we suddenly saw this used American-car showroom. 'Pull up, driver,' shouted Leslie with excitement, which is just what we did. A bit too quickly for my liking.

In no time at all Leslie had run into the showroom and was climbing in and out of all these huge American cars. The showroom's manager looked quite startled at this group of furry-headed young people with their trousers halfway up their legs. I think he thought the end of the world had come. Little did he think that day he would make a very good sale. Leslie came running back to me to report that at last he'd found a car that would both suit our needs and was mechanically in good condition.

We decided we'd buy it. It gave me a really funny feeling to pull out my cheque book and write out a cheque there and then for nearly £5,000. What a difference to a year or so back, when we were in debt for more than that amount.

Mind you, we'd had a very understanding bank manager in Mr. Dickson up in Prestonpans. Although he was in his late forties he seemed to understand what we were all about. Sometimes he showed the patience of a saint.

Our overdraft had been more than £5,000 at one time. I remember going in to see him when our records had at last started selling and saying: 'Well, it's really happening this time.' Suddenly I remembered that that was what I'd been telling him for the past few years. But he said he'd heard our records on the radio and that seemed to help a lot.

I think one of the essentials of becoming a successful group is having a patient and understanding bank manager with nerves of steel. After all, it wouldn't look very good for him if you'd borrowed all that money and then didn't succeed. But I think he somehow felt our enthusiasm. Anyway now we were able to sign a big cheque just like that without a worry.

It also made a lot of difference to the way the group worked. Sometime the National Insurance man had been knocking on the Longmuirs' door and asking: 'Could I speak to Alan Longmuir please.' Alan answered the door himself, and he'd say very quickly: 'Oh, I'm afraid he's down in London at the moment. He plays with a group and he stays in London.' The official from the insurance people would say, 'Well I'll come back and see him sometime next week.' That used to make Alan worry a lot because he'd be thinking all the time what he'd do when the man came back. When I used to drop down to their house he'd ask me: 'What am I going to say, what am I going to do?'

We did in fact owe about £700 in insurance stamps at the time, and the fact is that you can be sent to prison for owing a lot less than that. So you can see how these things could affect the group in all sorts of ways. Being a musician is just like having a job – you have to be free of worry to work really well. It's no good if you're mind is always ticking away asking you what you're going to say to the insurance man when next he knocks at the door.

And I think this is the background of worry and financial trouble that has made us very aware of the value of money.

This is another reason why our audience can identify with us more than with many other groups and stars. One of my theories has always been that The Rollers are a working man's group. In fact this feeling governs the places that we play.

I always reckon that kids would flock to see The Rollers from areas like Liverpool, and Manchester, Newcastle, Glasgow, and Edinburgh. When we went further south into England I was always worried, especially by places in the West Country like Taunton. I found that if we played in Conservative areas, things didn't work out very well for us.

In Labour areas everything seemed to go very well. We're not political, but this was just a fact of life that became evident to me at the time that I was trying to work out a booking pattern. Although The Rollers would draw a crowd anywhere they played today, I still have that feeling at the back of my mind that we are a working man's band. It's no good us doing gigs where people will be at all reserved. That is not our style, and it certainly is not our fans' style.

Then again a lot of people think that The Rollers are just a girls' group, but it's interesting to note that in the fan club one-third of our members are guys.

I've said before that the pressures of success can be just as great as, if not greater than, the pressure of struggling for success.

As we got even more successful people from outside tried to come between the group and myself. It's amazing that when we were on the way up, when we could have done with advice and help, there was none. I don't have a very high opinion of the London music business. I never had, because they'd always looked down on me as being the lad who brought his group down to London. They seemed to think that because we were based in Edinburgh, we knew nothing about our business. Well, they were wrong.

Now came the biggest bid to get rid of me. I was approached by a group of people who suggested that I sell them a share in The Rollers management. Of course I had to go to the group and tell them about it, because after all they might have wanted it. But in fact they threatened to break up if I gave away a part of the management, or the control of the group.

I was offered £60,000 for the management contract which I held. I was offered a wage to stay with the group. This is what I turned down because the group wanted things the way they had always been. And so did I. £60,000 is a lot of money even in these days of inflation, and it's as much as I'll probably ever earn, but that was not the point. I was so angered by people wanting to control The Rollers now that they were successful. Still, that is always the way in the music business in London.

About the same time I'd met up again with a very good friend, a person I'd liked for many years. He worked for an agency. He was called Barry Perkins. He left the agency and started working for me. I felt that he was taking quite a few of the pressures off me. We'd had a lot of hassles about various things like the musical direction the group should go in, and outside people had always considered me inexperienced. This was totally opposite to the view held by The Rollers themselves, but everyone always seems to know your business better than yourself.

I'd always had problems in getting outside people to see the way in which the group should go; in trying to convince them that my ideas were right. So there were a lot of conflicts and arguments. But when people actually tried to remove me from the management The Rollers themselves stepped in and said with one voice: 'Enough.'

The other major worry that was beginning to blow up behind the scenes now was the question of the 'B' sides on our records. Bill Martin and Phil Coulter had written and produced our most recent successes: 'Remember', which reached number six, 'Shang-a-Lang', which got to number two, and 'Summer Love Sensation', which made number three. These last two had been released in April and the July of 1974 and now Bell Records felt we should release one more for that year.

In fact Martin and Coulter came up with 'All Of Me Loves All Of You' which came out on October 4, 1974, and eventually reached number four. Our first album, 'Rollin', was released on September 6, 1974, and topped the album charts. So although we'd never actually had a number one single our first album made up for all that.

So Martin and Coulter had undoubtedly brought us a success, but they also demanded that they have the 'B' sides as well as the 'A' sides, and you earn just as much money from the 'B' sides as from the hits. This was beginning to frustrate me because I wanted the group to advance musically, and I always thought that if they did write a 'B' side it would give them a bit of encouragement. I'd always gone in to fight for them to have it, but I'd been defeated. The record company had said that eventually they would give us the 'B' side.

At the time we were on a low royalty with the record company. I think it was about five per cent, which meant that from each of 'Remember' and 'Shang-a-Lang' we would make about £5,000 profit. I really wanted to encourage the group in their writing because I felt that this was where their talents should develop in the future. I wanted them to have a good future, to be professional songwriters after the group finished. Just as I'd always be interested in Leslie going into acting if he fancied it, and I think he does.

I see the group lasting another five years. I hope they're going to be the biggest thing that has hit this country, because that's what I've always prayed for. After the five years is up, and even after my contract's up, even if they never re-sign with me again, I honestly want to see them do something in the business over the years. I see Eric and Woody writing a lot of songs. I see Leslie writing hit songs too. He's inclined to be a bit lazy at times, and I'm always telling him to get on with it. We've formed our own music publishing company, and I think that Derek is very clever at book-keeping.

He's very, very clever and I see him working in the business side of things. I think that Bay City Rollers Music will go on for years. I hope we'll be able to sign other acts too, and I can see Derek being interested in that side of things. But I can also see Derek as a very good session drummer playing with other musicians in the recording studios. I also think that he could move into producing records.

Bay City Music now owns all our songs, the ones that the group compose. Alan too is a fantastic bass player and he could be very valuable as a session man. He too would fit well into management in time to come. In fact I'd like Alan to come into management with me one day.

Sometimes The Bay City Rollers do worry about what they're all going to do in the future. This is only natural. I don't think there's anyone alive who doesn't worry about that at some time or another during their life.

Even I do that. I will continue in management, but as I've said, I see Alan joining me one day. I've served my apprenticeship in the business now, and I could teach him a lot about how the business works. He's also a very nice person and easy to get along with, and because of this he'd be an ideal person to work in management.

Still, all that is in the future. The mounting worry as we continued to succeed was to get the 'B' sides of the records for The Rollers' own work, so that at least they could progress from just being performers to being writers as well. And after 'All Of Me Loves All Of You' came out we felt that we really needed a change of producers. We'd had other producers before, starting with Jonathan King for 'Keep On Dancing' back in the early summer of 1971. We were very grateful to Martin and Coulter for what they'd done, but we felt we needed a change of writers as well. We appreciated that they had given us all these hits and I think they understood.

They understood that we needed a change of style, and the group wanted to do a bit of writing themselves, so we parted on a nice note, and that was it.

Bell Records had suggested another producer called Phil Wainman, who had worked with The Sweet among many other groups. Tony Roberts who was by now in Dick Leahy's position at Bell Records suggested Phil after he'd heard that we wanted a change.

Everybody in the music industry was a bit shocked when they heard that The Rollers had split with Martin and Coulter, and the people close to us at the record company were a bit worried. Here we were breaking up a successful partnership. But as I've said our first hit had been produced by Jonathan King, and we'd worked with other people as well.

So Tony Roberts at Bell got a few producers together and we went around them all and spoke to each one. Of them all we felt that Phil Wainman was the one for us.

What we really wanted was a producer, rather than a producer-songwriter, in order to leave the door open to our own material.

We never wanted every single, or 'A' side, to be written by one of The Rollers. We just want to have good singles, no matter who writes them. The first single we made with Phil Wainman in the session up at Chipping Norton studios was an old Four Seasons number called 'Bye Bye Baby'. It was out in America about ten years ago. We found that by sitting around in my place up in Scotland one night when all the boys were there. We went through about 2,000 singles and came across that one, and we thought: 'God that would make us a brilliant single.' So we don't want to write all our own material, neither do we want always to record one writer's material. It is much better to have a choice, because there is so much material around.

In fact on the 'B' side of that single Woody and Eric have a song of their own which is called 'It's For You', and I liked it a lot when they first played it to me.

We'll just keep our fingers crossed, but it's a start and that's all we wanted.

For our second album the Rollers have written several of the tracks themselves, and I think they sound very good. I'm a pretty harsh critic of their work, so they respect my opinion.

February, 1975, was to prove a very important month for The Bay City Rollers in many ways.

There were the daily recording sessions up at Chipping Norton for the new single and album. There was the debut of Eric and Woody as composers. Though they'd written stuff before they'd never actually had it recorded in the studio. We had a new producer in Phil Wainman, and now for the first time we were to meet a member of the Royal family, Princess Anne.

The occasion was the annual Carl Alan Award. The Mecca Agency rang us up several weeks before and told us that we'd probably win one of the awards. These are very important awards as far as the music business is concerned, and ten or more years ago the Best Group had been none other than the Beatles. Of course I was delighted and Mecca kept me in a state of suspense for some time. Eventually they rang again and said that we'd won the award as most popular group, and that Princess Anne would be presenting it to us.

It was an exciting night. The Rollers were wearing their new outfits, because we'd decided they wouldn't go in evening dress. Everyone else would be dressed that way, but The Rollers would neither feel nor look right in dinner jackets.

They would wear their new outfits, which they'd worked out with help of the designers and tailors, keeping their original style but just using a new trick here and there, like Leslie not having anything in tartan.

We all got ready at the hotel where we'd been staying for a month. And you've never seen so much excitement! You would have thought they were setting off for their first concert.

We drove up to the West End in a large black limousine. Outside the Empire Ballroom in Leicester Square there were all these crowds.

There was a certain amount of screaming as The Rollers arrived and went in the front door. And I must say that must be one of the few front doors we've been able to get through recently! But because of Royalty being present the security was very strict and there was no chance of the crowd breaking through and grabbing the boys.

I found it particularly exciting because soon after arriving I was speaking to one of the top men of the Mecca organization. He told me that he always knew when a group was going to be really big, because ever since the Beatles there had never been a group pestered for autographs. He didn't really think that The Bay City Rollers would be bothered by anyone that night. I permitted myself a secret smile. He said that The Beatles' manager, Brian Epstein, had placed a small bet with Mecca that The Beatles would be pestered for autographs. He won that bet, although no-one at the time thought they would be asked for anything. And I said that I'd also like to place a £1 bet on The Rollers being asked for their autographs. He readily agreed and told me, 'There's no way they'll be pestered at all. It's a very select audience, nobody will ask them.'

We never stopped signing autographs all night.

Princess Anne was very charming to the boys. She asked them where they were staying and Leslie piped up: 'Next door to you.'

That was a reference to the Royal Palace of Holyrood in Edinburgh. She said: 'I doubt that very much.' She asked them about their trousers, and Eric explained that as they bought their trousers on the never-never that was why they were only halfway down to their shoes. But when they'd paid up all the instalments they hoped their trousers would be the normal length.

The Princess stood and talked to The Rollers for quite a long time, saying things like: 'You've been obviously very successful this year.' The boys weren't nervous with her at all. In fact I think they geed her up a bit.

She was very nice and The Rollers were impressed. Alan told me afterwards that he really got a buzz when the Princess first came through the door and everyone stood up to receive her, and she wished him all the best for the coming year.

Derek actually took the award on behalf of the group and said a very proper 'Thank you very much.' I think she is really a very pleasant person, because when we were all having dinner I looked across to her table and she was obviously enjoying herself.

She enjoyed the cabaret that was provided, and I felt: 'I always enjoy myself at do's like that, and here she is enjoying herself.'

It was the fulfilment of an ambition for Alan, because although not all the guys like going to big functions (they feel it's not quite their thing) Alan admitted to me that he'd always wanted to go to something like this and here he was being presented to a member of the Royal family.

So in the end, despite all the initial worry and excitement it was a very successful night for The Rollers.

We're only halfway through 1975 by now but as I leaf through the memories in this book I feel that it should be called chapter one, because for The Bay City Rollers this is only the beginning.

OTHER GIANTS FROM BERKLEY

MORE BERKLEY BOOKS
YOU'LL WANT TO READ NOW